Critical Acclaim

Guido's Love, by David Kettlewell is a comforting, guileless and unpretentious book. It's a perfect read in a world that at times, seems anything but comforting or guileless. The writing is straightforward and original, sprinkled with imagery that transports the reader to Guido's childhood home and the sights, sounds, and smells of a small Italian farm in the 1940's.

Guido's childhood is rich without money and full without gluttony. The warmth of a loving family, the satisfaction of hard work well done and the beauty of the Italian countryside impart joys that transcend wealth, and as Guido matures and eventually immigrates to the US, he brings these values with him to his new home.

It's refreshing to use the word, "values." Sadly, this is a term that's been hijacked and to a degree, corrupted. Guido's Love speaks to real values, values of the heart and the spirit. Values that are learned from experience and love and not used as a political bludgeon. *Guido's Love* gently reminds the reader that there is such a thing as genuine, family values.

Kettlewell's book is essentially 5 different books, deftly woven together.

Life Story is about Italy and the rustic Italian countryside and family life on a farm. **Life Lessons and La Famiglia** speak to a loving, strong family. Then there's **Hair Care**. Yes, Hair Care! Guido's chosen profession is in a salon, and the inside perspective Kettlewell offers the reader is fascinating to anyone not affiliated with the hair care industry. Then there are **Recipes**...

The reader is allowed a glimpse of the sights and sounds and smells of a small, Italian indentured farm. Now the reader may experience the tastes on that farm with the inclusion of the family's precious recipes. This alone makes Guido's Love worth the purchase.

Finally, there's **The Fountain, or La Fontana:** A metaphor for dreams both realized and unfulfilled.

Kettlewell has written a book that is entertaining and enlightening and not at all preachy. It's an enjoyable read to be savored, hopefully with a nice glass of red wine, a piece of good bread and the warmth of family, whatever form that may be.

Kurt Niece

Kurt Niece writes about visual arts for SDGLN. He is a freelance journalist from Lakewood, Ohio. He is the author of "The Breath of Rapture" and soon to be published sequel, "Mercury Fields" and an artist who sells his work on knjewelry.com

GUIDO'S LOVE
Ways of Loving & Raising a Family That Work!

By David E. Kettlewell

Based on the life of Guido Cornacchione

FIRST EDITION
GUIDOSLOVE.COM
© David Kettlewell, 2013

ISBN: 1481065858

ISBN 13: 9781481065856

1~10~2017

To ESISA
con AMORE

WiTH LOVE

TABLE OF CONTENTS

LIFE LESSONS 129

Guido Cornacchione offers a wealth of practical wisdom based on a life well-lived, through short stories, each a jewel rich in meaning and application in your own life.

And count on Guido to serve it up old-world style-with a dash of humor, an Italian accent, and homemade red dolce wine. Con Amore!

LA FAMIGLIA *183*

Anecdotes from Guido's family, reflecting their take on love and life with Guido. Consider this your personal invitation to the Famiglia Cornacchione. Benvenuti a Casa!

With a long and decorated career as a renowned stylist, Mr. Guido offers the kind of expert hair care tips you simply cannot find elsewhere. Find recommendations for styles, cuts, processing color, and more. Served up with important life lessons. Che Bella!

RECIPES 287

The family's precious Italian recipes: cook like an Italian. *Mamma Mia!*

THE FOUNTAIN/LA FONTANA . . *311*

A short story connecting each of us with our unfulfilled dreams, where Vincenza's lifelong desire for "a three-tiered fountain" is fulfilled by her loving husband Guido. A testament that the Universe moves in quiet ways to complete our lives through love...at that moment when we least expect it.

·

FOREWORD

As time has passed, I've come to look at the ability to be in quality love relationships as a *skill*. Attraction is attraction, but the daily flow of a relationship is quite another thing.

As you read this story of Guido Cornacchione from a small farm town in Fossalto, Italy and his life in America, you will find a man with a sublime understanding of how to love his family...how to make them *feel* his love, *know* his love, and *count on* his love.

It is a reflection of his family upbringing, which we catalog in detail, and an approach to family and customers we can all learn from.

Interspersed with this are tips on hair care, and as you might guess, hair stylists know more about people than most of us!

For me personally, each interview over a 5 year period was an eye opener. We toiled on the book together over homemade dolce wine and his wife Vincenza's Italian cooking. You'll even find the family's recipe treasures here to enjoy.

If your reaction to this book is like mine in writing it, you will find inspiration in its stories and come away with a new understanding of how to love others.

This book is dedicated to my mother, Barbara Kettlewell, an author of short stories and one captivated by fine writing. Many a day and evening were spent reading each other books and discussing what we thought they meant. Whatever focus I possess as a writer certainly comes from her, and our hours submerged in classics and discussions of same.

Of course, this book is also dedicated to my father, breadwinner extraordinaire with artistic flair. (Although that flair may be partially due to the influence of MaryJane Stanchina- I'll think about that!), and of course, to Jane, top-notch caregiver for Pop & honorary family member.

Good hunting as you seek for the keys to deeper love relationships in your own life, and I hope you find Guido to be the marvelous inspiration I have found him to be.

David E. Kettlewell, author

DEDICATION

This book is dedicated to my brother, Frank, and his wife Carmela Cornacchione, without whose support I would not have been able to come to America, and thus much of this story would never have happened.

And of course, in remembrance of my mother and father, and my entire family.

One of the concerns I had when initially thinking about creating a book was that I believed the only persons who could understand my life in Italy and write about it with some accuracy would be those who were there, who actually saw what happened.

David Kettlewell, the researcher and author, surprised me in his ability to make the places and happenings come alive as if he were actually there. One time, he called to read me a chapter where my mother gave me a leather pouch with remembrances when I left home. David had made it up. He read me the passage, "But David, that is exactly what happened!" He had never heard this story, but his imagination had guessed right! Grazie Davide!

—Guido Cornacchione (Mr. Guido)

ILLUSTRATIONS

Artist Mike Blanc

The illustrations for *Guido's Love* were created by illustrator, Mike Blanc.

Mike works for Artists, Incorporated in Akron, Ohio. He lives nearby with his wife Gail in Doylestown, Ohio where he enjoys art appreciation and collecting vinyl records. He has 4 children and 5 grandchildren. Mike's children's book titles include Moonbeam Award Gold Medal winners: *Bonyo Bonyo, The True Story of a Brave Boy from Kenya*, with Kristin Blackwood and *I Came From the Water, One Haitian Boy's Incredible Tale of Survival*.

TIMELINE FOR GUIDO CORNACCHIONE'S LIFE

Born on Nov. 9th, 1938 in Fossalto, Italy at the home farm. Son of Emilio & Nicoletta Cornacchione.

Birth of Vincenza Ciraldo, (Guido's future wife) August 9th, 1940.

Left farm for a larger farm in Russi, Italy, May of 1959

Left Italy for England to be a cook, Feb., 1962

Met the Beatles, May, 1962

First visit to United States Nov. 10th, 1963

Met Vincenza, his future wife, May, 1964

Engaged to Vincenza, daughter of Alfio and Nunzia Ciraldo of Sicily, November of 1964

Married to Vincenza, Jan. 2, 1965

Birth of son Emilio Cornacchione Nov. 18, 1968

Birth of son Carlo Cornacchione, Nov. 17th, 1970

Birth of daughter Lisa Cornacchione, May 16th, 1973

Birth of daughter Rita Cornacchione, July 21st, 1974

(Guido Corn-ahh-key-ohnay is the way the name is pronounced... actual spelling is Cornacchione)

LIFE STORY

MORNING IN AMERICA

Guido lay next to his wife, Vincenza, and listened as her soft, gentle breathing accompanied the rise and fall of the cream-colored sheets. He opened his right eye and coursed his hand not more than half an inch from her face, following the curvature of her well-shaped brow, then touching her nose and lips with his fingertip.

Watching her, he could not help but think that it was an invasion of her privacy, yet, how can it be an invasion when it's your own wife of 30+ years?

Once again, his dreams had been of his boyhood, and parents' farm wrapped in the gentle waves of land in Fossalto, Southern Italy- a world where each year's toil left them no real profit of any kind, beyond the riches of a life full of a family's love.

Again, he saw the images as clear as a motion picture in his mind of the color of the golden sun on the undulating hills; of him and his brothers working the soil morning to night by hand with hoes, rough burlap cloth wrapped around their shoe tops to keep the dirt from falling into their shoes.

Of the cold nights with no heat, and apples under the bed. Of the rabbit cages with their dry wooden posts all a kilter, hung with chicken wire. Of a time before he'd come to America, before he'd built a successful marriage and career and built a home considered a wealthy man's estate were it in Italy.

Of sitting on his Grandmother's lap while her weathered fingers rubbed his ears between her thumb and fingers, and her coo, "little

Guido, you always can count on your good looks," the squeeze of his cheeks, and her words, "bene, bene," in his ear as she kissed him over and over until both his cheeks were wet with her kisses.

His eyes closed and he fell into a light sleep again in the grey mists, thinking of his favorite cow as a child, his little Fiorentina.

MORNING IN FOSSALTO, ITALY

Guido's eyes popped open in the darkness, just ahead of the sunrise, although this morning, as most mornings, he would pretend to sleep while his two brothers lying on either side of him in the bed would wake in turn, and shake off the piercing cold of November.

November's cold and howling wind and the light snows that would melt soon after sunrise, and evenings of warmed wine.

His fingers would be colder now, and he might wear his hat, but not the warm coat handed down from two brothers he would wear in December and January.

Guido's rich dark hair pushed into the pillow made of goose down, and he'd placed a blue-grey hand towel over his head and tucked around his neck to stay warmer. 'I look like a sheik," he thought.

His two brothers were still asleep. Guido, age 8, listened to the soft muted breathing of Teodoro, his older brother, lying to his right. At 16, Teodoro enjoyed the pick of the best jobs on the farm, like guiding the donkey loaded with ground flour back from the mill (he got to go all by himself) or holding the plow handle like Papa did, although his mamma told him, "Guido, it's not easier work, but you must be more mature for those jobs."

"What is mature?" he asked, but his mamma fell silent and kept feeding the fire.

He was sitting on his grandmother's lap when she said it while stroking his ears gently, "Guido, he always want to be better, you gonna be somebody, he gonna be somebody. He's the smart one, you see."

27

A jab, Liberato's foot kicked him again in bed. Age 10 and to Guido's left, Liberato kicked every half hour, all night long. Guido had even timed it once, but it didn't bother him any more than the creaky noise the barn door made every time you opened it.

"How can it be that rich people sleep one to a bed?," thought Guido, "How do they stay warm?"

Even with the three in the bed lying close like kittens they would just be warm enough on the cold nights. The only room with heat was the kitchen, and the fire was just starting.

"Why should I want to get up before Mamma has the fire going?"

It was a fine bedroom, Guido thought as the dawn's light reflected on the whitewashed walls with paint made from white rocks fire burned and pulverized from the Quarry, mixed by Mr. Sonabito and sold in cans which they painstakingly spread each three years on every stick of wood on the farm with brushes made from horse tails.

In two years, Papa says I can paint the walls instead of feeding the fire, where your hands and arms ache from the heat and you can't breathe from the smoke.

Soon he would be in the kitchen, after pretending to be asleep of course, while his two brothers would rise to prepare for the day's work.

He had a system. First, you pretend to be asleep as the others get up to begin getting dressed. Then, when Papa calls, you make a small move like you're going to get up- enough so the brothers see.

Then, the two brothers go downstairs and Papa asks, "Where is Guido?" "He's coming," they reply. Then, this is the good part, you lie down again and roll the covers all around you until Papa or Teodoro come up to get you.

I hope it is Papa, because Teodoro will crack me on the head or the ribs, while Papa would just take my face in his hands and say, "I'm on to you, I give it to you...you got this far, but if you don't get up right now I will tickle you until you cry, and your mamma won't be able to stop me. I mean it this time," accompanied by a mimed stern look.

Then Guido would hug him and make his Papa lift him up and set him on the floor, and oh, the floor would be soooo cold.

"Your mamma has the fire going, so get down quick so your feet don't freeze," said his papa, who accepted his life on the farm where it *felt* like you faced an endless flow of farming to an ever-receding horizon...day after day of sweat, dust, and toil.

Guido slid on his clothes, all handmade of the best cloth they could find from his brothers' older clothing, and peered out the window to see the chimney smoke rising from a nearby home.

Guido still did not understand...he had heard the man at the neighbor's house, the one who got kicked by his own mule, whispering with his wife once, and saying that Guido's father, "would never amount to much."

"He didn't go to school, he never amount to anything in life." Then his wife's voice stopped whispering, and she loudly said while slapping her thigh with the spatula, "There's much you could learn from that man who has a family who loves him and a wife who thinks he's God, and not sons who steal like yours."

The man's wife would give Guido hugs and the little breadsticks when he was visiting. But the husband would keep a distance and walk away if Guido got close, like a shy stray cat.

"Someday, I'll understand," Guido said to himself, which is what his grandmother always told him, "someday you'll understand."

DEAR NONNA

Dear Nonna,

I am writing this for my 3rd grade class. I hope my teacher likes it.

Every morning I get up early before the sun is up to feed our two cows, Fiorentina and Marinella.

I love Fiorentina, but I don't love Marinella.

Fiorentina likes me to scratch her ears and likes me to pat her. Her hair is white and light tan, and I tell her what happens to me each day.

Marinella is not a nice cow. She tried to chase me once when she got away from me, and kick me once and I don't trust her.

In the morning, I go under our house where the cows live and get the milk bucket and sit on the stool with my head touching the cow.

Then I milk the cows one at a time. I use my fingers to pull on the cow's menna (teats), and milk spurts out against the metal bucket.

Sometimes the milk goes onto the dirt floor, but not very much.

One day I spilled the milk and Mamma said to be more careful.

Fiorentina is my friend but I don't trust Marinella.

Marinella's eyes are like a shark, black and mean. She is waiting to kick me.

But Fiorentina is my friend, and she has never kicked me.

I give treats to Fiorentina and a little to Marinella.

I think Marinella needs to go to school to learn to be a better cow.

Goodbye Nonna, I'll see you tonight.

Your Guido

THE DRUNK COW

In the pecking order of the family farm work, feeding the cows seemed just right to little Guido.

You had to be old enough to handle the cows and not let them push you around, but it wasn't as backbreaking as working the fields day after day in the summer heat, where your whole body was wet with sweat, and your feet suffered the little bits of stones and dirt in your shoes all day...where the sun moved so slowly across the sky, and all you had to dream about was to wait for the little lunches of bread, cheese, wine and perhaps a fig wrapped in cloth, brought to you by your sister, which you'd eat in the field sitting on a pile of dirt.

Guido's hand touched Fiorentina's rump, "You are my good little Fiorentina," said Guido, as he walked his fingers along her body, across her back and then tummy and neck to her ears which he grasped in his little hands and rubbed on the inside with his thumbs until her eyes closed. "Have I got a little surprise for you."

Today was the day when the two cows (the good cow, Fiorentina, and the very bad cow, Marinella) got to drink the wine mash- a glop of leftover grapes and bits of stems and alcohol left over from the bottom of the wooden wine vats.

"You put a little in the bucket," he told her just like his papa had told him two years ago, as he grasped the wooden bucket bigger than he was around the waist, with it's 2 rusting metal bands, and ladled in about a gallon of glop.

Then he took the bucket and filled it to about 3 inches from the top with water.

"You're my good little Fiorentina," he told her as he unhooked her tether from the stall under the house, and led her to her bucket of glop by the cistern which collected all the rain from the roof of the house.

He did not hook the T-shaped metal bar into the cistern's rusting O ring, because she was always good. He patted her rump again and pulled her tail a little bit until she looked at him with the big black eyes that said, "you are my friend, little Guido."

Guido looked back at the house and "The Little Pig," his name for Marinella ever since she tried to run him over.

"She almost killed me, her eyes were mean, she was after me," he had told his mamma as she was baking bread one day. He walked around the kitchen with the chair in his hands showing her how Marinella pushed him and how she had tried to take the piece of candy in his pocket. "She wanted to kill me," he said excitedly.

Mamma shook her head, and looked at him, "She's just a cow."

He filled Marinella's smaller bucket with the wine mash, making sure it was a little less than he gave to his sweet Fiorentina, and then walked to the cistern, adding the water and set the bucket down.

"I will have to tether Marinella, because she is a bad cow," said Guido under his breath as he walked to "The Little Pig," trying to figure out how she might try to kill him today.

"You are a mean cow, but I'm gonna give you the wine mash anyway, because Mamma says you'll make more milk. But be good or you'll be in trouble and have to sit on the chair in the front of the class," said Guido, in the same voice his teacher used with the kids each day in the one room schoolhouse attached to the house nearby, with its wood stove on the raised platform only the teacher got to sit near, with all the kids around her in a semi-circle, their little feet near the stove.

Guido carefully led Marinella, but first he looked her dead in the eye and said, "Be good, or I'll tell on you."

"Fiorentina! Stop it!," Guido cried as he saw his sweet cow had finished her own bucket and was now diving into the bucket prepared for Marinella.

"You only get one...stop it, stop it!," he cried.

Guido did not know what to do, he pushed on her rump, and pushed on her shoulder, but she would not move. He pulled on her tail, sloppy gulping sounds were the only response.

"This is not good," he said. He grabbed her aged and cracked leather lead line and pulled as hard as he could.

"You are too big," he told her, poking her ribs with his fingers.

He didn't know what to do, so he let go of the lead line and backed away, sat on the ground, and watched- his face cradled between his hands.

She finished all the mash, with huge sucking sounds, now two buckets full total, and turned to look at Guido. The red mash and water ran out of her mouth and nose and she looked at him like a crazed monkey.

Then, her ears stood straight up, Guido had never seen this before.

Her tail stood straight up like a flagpost, Guido had never seen this before.

Then she farted, which Guido had heard many times.

She farted again and sauntered out of the barn like a drunk princess, a hippopotamus of the Italian plains.

"Stop, you gonna be a bad cow!," said Guido as he ran back to put Marinella's iron T into the iron ring of the cistern. "You're the good cow today," he said as he patted her nose.

Fiorentina, who used to be the good cow- but now had transformed into the bad cow- ran faster and faster down the drive with Guido running after her, his shoes still untied.

Faster and faster she ran, and Guido ran harder too. Then his one shoe fell off, and he didn't know whether to go back for the shoe and tie them both, or run after her quick. He just ran fast.

"I'm gonna get into trouble for this," thought Guido.

"You are gonna be a bad cow," he cried as the two ran on and on and on down the road past the little bushes and the broken farm tool, and farther to where the frogs lived and where the dead dog was found 3 years ago.

Finally, she turned right into a wet muddy field. Guido cried, "No, don't go, turn right, don't go in there you bad cow."

She sunk like a beached ship into the mud, inch-by-inch, gloppy brown wet mud, a sea of ooze...all the way up to her knees. Then she looked at Guido and her wildness was gone.

"I'm not gonna come down there cause it's too muddy, and I have my shoe on and it will ruin it, so you have to figure out how to get outta there."

He sat down on the road and cradled his head in his hands.

After a couple of minutes he thought he should go home because he still needed his breakfast.

"I'm gonna go home and tell Mamma what you did."

He walked slowly up the road towards the house, thinking of what he would tell her.

He thought about many things he could say, but decided he'd just say Fiorentina had been drinking too much like Uncle Billoni and was stuck in the mud," and see how it went from there.

He wasn't sure he'd say anything about the ring and the T, maybe they wouldn't ask.

I wonder what Mamma made for breakfast, he thought as the house came into view.

Later that day, 6 members of his family struggled to pull the cow from the mud.

Guido took her to the cistern and washed her legs, put her in her stall and rubbed her ears before going into supper. "Be a good cow from now on, ok?"

"It's an Electric Cat!"

THE ELECTRIC CAT *part one*

Little Guido felt the warmth of summer against his cheek as he left the house to feed the rabbits after breakfast, "If it's this hot so early in the morning, it's going to be very hot today," he thought.

It was not a bad job to feed the rabbits. They were soft, they didn't bite, and Guido treated them like pillows, snuggling his nose into their soft fur. Sometimes he would take his favorite, Sparky, on walks and talk with her about all the animals on the farm. "This is Marinella, she is a bad cow because..."

Guido fed Fiorentina her usual mash with water (she was now back in his good graces after the wine mash episode), and looked at her right eye which had been tearing, and wiped what was left of yesterday's tears from her face. She was not a pretty cow, but she was healthy, and he was glad he would not have to ask Papa to bring the vet because it cost too much.

He walked to the rabbit pen area just inside the barn doors and it took a moment for the picture to register.

Sparky was dead and lying next to her like sticks all pointed in the same direction were three other rabbits, including the white one with the black spot around its eye.

Guido picked up Sparky and put her on his lap. She was limp and so had not been dead long. "It's that damn cat, that stinking no good stray cat," he whispered as he cried and patted Sparky.

For the first time in his life, revenge boiled in little Guido's heart. It surged through him like a boiling oil till he almost shook. His eyes narrowed and lips pursed, fed by the loss of Sparky and his general dislike of cats and anything that bites including snakes, bugs, and bad dogs.

"Stinky cats!," Guido intoned. As Grandpa had said, "watch out for anything with no friends."

Grandpa had told him how bad stray cats would kill rabbits for fun-first one, then another, killing for sport, not even eating one. Once the cat developed a taste for the sport, it would keep on killing.

Now four beautiful rabbits were dead, just as Grandpa had said.

"You're gonna be sorry cat," he whispered.

Guido slid two 16 gauge shotgun shells into the rust-pitted shotgun Grandpa had given him. He knew exactly how to open it, push down the little lever behind the trigger, how to cock it open, how to push the two shells side-by-side all the way in, then close the gun with a "snap" because it's a little hard to close, and put on the safety with a "click."

"What are you doing?," Mamma asked as she threw the feed and leftover breadcrumbs to the chickens, and spied the gun in his hands through the barn door.

He pointed to the four rabbits.

She came in the barn and saw the four animals, laid out like sticks.

"So you think you're going to shoot the cat that killed the rabbits?"

He nodded.

"Guido, your father needs to shoot the cat. They are hard to hit, and if you don't kill them, they run and hide and stink up the barn. Let your papa kill the cat."

She saw Sparky in his lap, and saw a look in his eyes she had not seen before. "He is growing up," she said to herself, and then, "let him be a little man today."

"Well, if the cat runs we'll look for blood," then she picked up the four rabbits to take to the kitchen. They would have meat tonight.

"Aren't we going to bury Sparky?," Guido asked, his eyes teary.

He watched his mother walk to the house.

"I have seen this cat once," said Guido to himself. He often pretended his best friend from school, Toni, was with him. He'd pose questions for Toni, then answer them himself.

"What color is it?" Guido asked, pretending to be Toni.

"The cat is orange, orange and yellow, with yellow eyes."

"What are you going to do to the cat?" asked Toni.

"You will see."

All day he sat with the gun in the barn, waiting. Nothing. Just the animals and the occasional fly he swatted away. "I wish it were not so hot. When Mamma comes I'll ask her for some water."

"I'm going to have to figure this out better," he thought as he spied the wooden crates around him.

He looked overhead and remembered the stray cat liked to walk on the roof beams, each a heavy wooden squared off pole cut from the trees by the pond, or so his papa had said.

Last summer, he climbed on them to help fix the roof, and knew they had a quarter inch of grey dust on them.

And then he remembered seeing cats walk on them before, and if the sun came in just right, you'd see a cloud of dust sparkle in the light with each step.

Guido looked and thought, "If I stay where I am, and shoot in this direction, I'm going to put a hole in the roof and I'll get into trouble with Papa."

"But if I shoot this way, then when the cat jumps from one beam to the next...then the shot will go out to the sky, missing the roof."

"You think you're gonna shoot that cat and miss the barn, do you Guido?," said his imaginary friend.

"I'm going to hide," he said to himself as he slid the 3 foot high wooden crate with the broken jar inside across the dirt floor to where the old concrete slabs with the big yellow and white pebbles in them started, facing it away from where he thought the cat would come.

Then Guido dragged a second crate and faced it toward the barn door, the two crates' backs against each other for support, making a little space for him to shoot from.

"I'll sit in the crate facing the barn door, and the cat won't see me here."

He grabbed the old blue and red wool blanket speckled with wood shavings...the one with the tiny holes in it from mouse nibbles, (used to cushion the wagon seat before the wagon wheel had broken), and placed it on the floor of the first crate, then climbed in.

His full weight pushed against the crate and it was stable. But the gun felt heavy, and his arms were getting tired.

Then he dragged over two sacks of corn feed used for cows. "I'll lay my gun on the sacks."

And there he sat, for hours, not moving a muscle. Waiting, waiting, waiting, for the cat.

As the last light of the day was peering through the barn door, his mamma came in with a basket.

"Guido, where are you?"

He answered from his spot. "You have to find me."

"I can't see anything, where are you?"

"I'm in the crates."

She looked at the crates and the blanket and the sacks.

"Why are you hiding?"

"So the cat won't see me," he said.

"I brought you your dinner, some bread, and cheese, and a little wine, and..." she said nothing of the freshly cooked rabbit on the plate.

She watched him eat, and wasn't sure if she really wanted him to shoot the cat, or not.

"Are you going to stay out here all night?"

"Yes. I am going to kill the cat."

"Your papa is late. He's at the mill helping Mr. Thampsio, the farmer with the bad hand."

She watched him eat, and walked back to the house.

Guido forced his eyes open, then his head bobbed down and up and he would just fall to sleep...then wake with a slight quiver of his body. At about midnight, he heard his papa's footsteps on the gravel and heard the door of the house close.

It was a fitful night. He'd sleep a bit, then wake to hear the sounds of summer…little mice feet scampering on the floor, the breathing and snorting of the cows, and the crickets outside. Once he heard something and the crickets stopped, but it went away and the cricket song resumed.

He could barely make out the rafters against the night sky. It was a quarter moon with clouds, and it reminded him of the time he had to walk back home from the mill with his papa in the dark, and the coolness of the wet summer evening, when he could just see the ground. "It's not hard to find your way at night, Guido, you can see the path."

"Walk slowly, your eyes adjust. See, it's just like daytime, just less light." He remembered the smells, the freshness of everything at night on the path, and later the dew and the cool air against his skin.

But it was warm in the barn and he was not alone. He knew the animals all wanted the cat dead, especially the rabbits still in the pen.

He had to pee, so got up and went over to the rabbit pen and picked up one of the babies. He held it and stroked its chin and pushed its wet nose against his cheek. He felt wetness on his arm. "You peed on me, why did you pee on me?," he said quietly. "Back you go to bed."

When dawn came, he was fast asleep and slumped in the crate. The gun lay against the sack to the left, arms crossed against his body to help him stay warm.

He awoke and opened his sleepy eyes, then saw a movement and looked up to see the stray killer cat walking on the beam overhead, stalking like a hungry lion, intent on killing another rabbit. "You murderer, now is your time to pay for Sparky," he thought. The cat paused, motionless, thinking about jumping to the next beam.

Then it dawned on him, "I don't have the gun in my hands, how could I be so stupid? Now I have to pick up the gun, pull off the safety, aim, and shoot. How could I be so stupid?"

"All I had to do was stay awake, and I could have just pulled the trigger. See what a mess I'm in. How could I do this?"

He thought about everything that could go wrong. He might knock over the gun, or miss, or forget to release the safety like happened to uncle Mario with the deer and everybody laughed each year at the story being told.

"Why didn't you stay awake? If the cat sees you and runs away, all your waiting and dragging the crates and tired arms will be for nothing," his imaginary friend said.

He thought hard. "Just think everything through and do it smooth and fast. Exactly what do I have to do?"

First, he had to grab the gun...he'd take his right hand to grab the stock, slide his hand to the trigger, then support the barrel with his left hand, raise the gun and aim while pushing off the safety, and....fire, and hit the cat.

He pictured each movement in his mind over and over, staring at the cat as it stood frozen on the beam...deciding whether to jump or no.

Just wait...wait...wait.

After one minute that seemed like one hour, the cat leapt...

Guido saw the cat in the air, saw its body arch in the air as its front paws hit the beam, its rear legs coming under its body.

Guido did not really think. His body took over like the time he threw the stone at the crow and hit it.

It just "happened." The gun was in his hands, he raised it to the cat, the "click" of the safety being released, lining up the cat and barrel and squeeze of the trigger slowly...slowly to be accurate....slow like a knife sliding through butter.

"Boom," and everything in the barn jumped.

The cows mooed and the chickens scampered, and the rabbits scurried and squealed, and Guido found that he was on his back. The crate had tipped over and he'd tumbled out.

Running to the barn door he looked for the cat. It was gone, no cat. "You missed, ha ha ha, all this waiting and you missed," said his imaginary friend.

There was no blood on the floor and no pellets in the wood. Again, "You missed."

"It's impossible, I shot him, I know I did."

He walked outside the barn and looked to the right, then he looked to the left and saw the cat's body peppered with buckshot. The blood on the ground was in a swirling shape, the cat must have been spinning when it fell.

His mamma and papa ran down the stairs to the lower level of the house and out by the side door.

"Did you hit him? Good shot Guido! What are you going to do with him?"

"I'm going to skin him." Guido spent the entire day on the project. First, he skinned the cat and gutted the cat, and threw the innards to where the wild animals could take them away from the house so they'd have something to eat too.

Then he turned the skin inside out and tacked the skin to a board to dry and rubbed in small bits of rock salt to cure it.

Three weeks went by and each day he would lecture the dead cat, standing before it, "You killed Sparky and see what happened to you. Now you are a dead cat and won't kill Sparky again."

But anger subsided and he got to know the little rabbit that peed on him and it was when walking with his new baby rabbit with no name that the idea first hit him. He had been looking at the sky...and it dawned on him.

"The Man with the Big Moustache"

THE ELECTRIC CAT part two

The boards were old and grey and weathered from sitting behind the barn, with bird droppings running down their length and a small crack 5 inches long.

"This will do," said Guido.

He took the old hammer with the broken claw and the hacksaw, and using old pipes and spare bits of wood and metal, he cut and smoothed and hammered until he'd created a weathervane in the shape of a small airplane.

Five feet long from front to tail, with a little steering wheel from the old baby buggy in the trash heap suspended by what had been a baby wheel axel, with a propeller made from the thin slats of wood from some crates, angled so they would turn with the wind.

The board with the crack would do for the plane's tail piece, "It will work just as well," said Guido.

Guido scampered into the barn moving more quickly than normal, and looked at the skin with a head on the board that had been the stray cat.

He pulled the skin from the board. It was stiff, so he found the smelly thick brown mule hoof goop and slopped it on the skin, rubbing it in with a rag which he threw away because the goop smelled so bad, and left it to soak for half an hour.

Finding the cat pelt soft enough, Guido stuffed the skin with straw, sewing it shut with the twine and needle used to fix the grain sacks.

"What are you doing?," yelled his brother Domenico as he saw Guido climb to the highest peak of the house close to his papa and mamma's room.

"You will see," said Guido.

He nailed a 4 foot galvanized pipe piece to the side of the house, and wiggled it to see if it was strong enough to withstand a strong wind.

It was, so he clambered down and labored up the ladder with the plane to see how it all might work.

It would clear the house as it swung, but it needed something to pivot on.

He laid the plane down on the roof, clambered down, and after a half an hour found a broken hinge from a door with a 3 inch post left attached, then climbed up the ladder again and screwed the broken hinge a bit forward of the plane's mid-balance point.

He inserted the pin in the pipe, and the weathervane worked. It was a bit heavy and cumbersome, and there was hardly enough wind, but it did line up with the direction of the light breeze and the blades turned slowly.

"You're making a windmill," said his brother while eating an apple.

Guido nodded.

The stuffed cat was carried up the ladder dangling by his stiff foot and Guido pushed the arms and body into the shape of a pilot, with its paws on the steering wheel.

Guido climbed down to review his work, and saw it was not complete.

He hunted and hunted and found the old spraying goggles with a crack in the lens and missing headband. He put holes in the goggle sides with an old nail and hammer, and climbed to attach them with wire to the stuffed cat's head.

"It looks like a flying cat," said Domenico, "but Papa won't let you keep it up there," then went looking for Papa to prove his point.

His papa looked up at Guido and the cat and the plane, and laughed so hard that tears came out of his eyes. Domenico said, "You're not going to let him leave that thing up there, are you?"

Papa just laughed and laughed, and even slapped his thigh.

Mamma came out, saw the plane but just looked at Guido, but Guido thought he saw a slight smile on her face.

"You're not going to leave that thing up there, are you?," Domenico repeated.

Everyone who came to the farm saw the cat and darned if it didn't look like the cat was flying the plane.

Guido always thought it was the goggles which made the best finishing touch...that was his favorite part.

The story was told time and again in the small town of Fossalto, and each visitor to the farm stared and would not move until they heard the whole story.

It was told over wine and homemade cheese with coarse white bread, sometimes with pickled peppers, with much laughter. Was told again and again and entered the folklore of the village along with the stories including the drunk priest who walked his goat with the leash, even when the goat had wiggled free and escaped.

One time, a city man came to the farm with a big white and grey moustache that extended past his face an inch on each side. He looked up and asked Guido about the cat.

Guido said that the cat ran the electricity on the farm, and that was how they got the two lightbulbs on the farm to light. "It's an electric cat!"

The man thought for a moment, then laughed and laughed and Guido told him the true story, and even showed him the little generator that fed the lights.

The man with the big moustache took a liking to Guido, and told him many of his best jokes, even the one about the woman called, "La Gorda," with the zucchini, which Guido thought would get him into trouble with Papa so he never told anyone that story.

When the man with the big moustache was leaving, he said, "I have a little gift for you," and he gave Guido a tiny knife so small even Guido's hands could hardly open it.

"A man can never have too many good jokes. Remember that little Guido!"

Two years later, Guido's papa was telling the story at a party, and it had grown in length somewhat over time, with some additions Guido knew were not really accurate but made the story better.

"And no stray cat ever killed another rabbit from the barn," said his papa while he hugged Guido's head and patted his dark hair. Guido twisted his head around to those in the room saying, "it's an Electric Cat."

EMILIA AND HER "GOD GIVEN BEAUTY"

Emilia was short and fat with portly legs and white blanched skin with reddish blonde hair. She was disliked because she smacked the hands of the boys who wanted to go pee during class with a ruler, but in her defense this was only because the boys were going out to play, not pee, and she didn't know what else to do.

And so, as often happens, the boys decided to get their revenge in ways only little boys can do.

The simple one room schoolhouse measured about 20 feet by 14 feet, and its resemblance to a large living room was no accident, as it had been built by the owner of the home to which it was attached, of white block quarry stone.

It was built for the owner's mother who wanted privacy after her adopted son by her first marriage was left on the field with 100,000 other Italian troops when the German army had "requisitioned" all their trucks to enable the German troops to flee from the Russians pushing westward to avenge Stalingrad and take Berlin near the end of World War II.

"How could the Germans take our trucks and leave our children to the Russians? What did they think the Russians would do to our men?"

But then the owner's mother had died of a failing heart and the owner decided to lease the room as a schoolhouse, followed by a large lunch for the town officials for which he had to pay and a gift for each, and this one room became the new schoolhouse for the 20 children.

It was painted white, not insulated in the least, uncomfortable and hot in the summer, lacking adequate windows and screens...but even more uncomfortable in winter time when the drafts were merciless and the cold incessant in December, when the snow was more frequent and the winds howled at night.

Although one change had been made to assist the boys' and girls' comfort, which was to add a raised section of brick on one end of the room upon which sat a pot bellied stove fed by wood brought and stacked by Leone, the caretaker of the school (room) whose son Pisone, the one with a learning disability, received extra attention.

Behind the stove sat the teacher's large dark wooden desk whose left drawer had lost its hardware, so she opened it by sticking a pen in and pulling...and in front, on cold days, the teacher would sit in a chair with the stove to her back, and the children would sit in front of her in a semi-circle.

The boys were at the very front of this semi-circle, and she would look at them with their dark straight hair and beautiful skins, and wonder if they would grow up to break women's hearts by promises of marriage unfulfilled.

"I want you to read your papers on what you did yesterday. Guido you go first."

Guido rose and looked to his friends for support. They liked Guido, so just cocked their heads and puckered their lips, but did not make noises like they might do for one less popular.

"Yesterday, I got up in the morning and fed the cows and the chickens and Mamma had breakfast, then I went to school and then I worked in the field harvesting the wheat with my brothers."

"What is the matter with you? This is exactly the same what you wrote two days ago when I gave this assignment! Why do you write the exact same thing, are you trying to make me mad?"

"No, I do the same thing every day, really. I get up, feed the cows and the chickens and eat and go to school and work on the wheat. And then when the wine comes in, I will work the grapes until they are done. But that won't happen for 6 months."

Guido knew that this was not what she wanted to hear, and his sister had warned him not to write the same thing two days in a row as it would only cause trouble, but Guido said, "She asked us to write what we do that day, and it's the same thing!"

"If you do the same thing each day you write about it different!," she said as she smacked his shoulder with the ruler.

Paolo saw it first. When the teacher spread her legs he could see her baggy loose white cotton underwear with the long slit to allow her to relieve herself without disrobing in the winter cold, and on occasion her "God Given Beauty," would be visible too which Paolo also saw on his sister.

This was shared with the other boys, and the teacher was pleased to see that the next day they leaned in more than ever to hear her speak. "They are learning not to be such animals," she said to herself, and, "I will teach them to be better boys than to promise a young woman marriage, kiss her, and then run off with a prettier girl."

It was that day that Paolo really had to go pee and asked to go outside. She said, "You know what you get, come get the ruler on your hand." But today he had said without thinking, "I really have to go pee and I don't think I should be hit with a ruler. Just let me go pee."

She hit his palm so hard that he peed his pants a little, which the others did not notice, and when he peed outside tears fell from his cheeks which he wiped off carefully.

Paolo took his seat and Guido noticed that his eyes were wet, that he smelled a little of urine, and saw the red welt on his hand. Guido was not as close to Paolo as he was with some of the other boys, but decided to be nicer to him as they were united in dislike of the ruler hitter.

Paolo saw her God Given Beauty again later that afternoon, and it was then that his plan was hatched.

She was eating her snack of a raw egg, where she would prick a hole in the top and bottom of the egg, sprinkle salt in the top hole, then placing her lips on the lower hole, tilt her head back and suck the contents of the egg slowly into her mouth...when his hand sprung up and he smacked her God Given Beauty.

It was the equivalent of hitting a wasp's nest; she dropped her egg which broke on the bricks and grabbed him by the ear, taking him outside to hit him with "the board".

Paolo pushed his face to her hair and said in her ear while shaking, "If you touch me, or ever smack my hand again with the ruler when I have to pee, I will tell my father, and his brother who ran the prison will come to you and he will break your jaw."

Guido expected Paolo to come back to his seat, if at all with welts on his face, but he saw none.

Emilia spoke with many people in the town later that day, and learned that the brother had served as a prison guard during the war but none would say exactly what he had done to certain prisoners because it was "best forgotten and not spoken of," and even this was said only in hushed whispers.

The next day in class Emilia said, "From now on you can only go out to pee when you really have to pee, and I will decide who is lying and the liars will get the ruler."

But she never hit Paolo again, and even treated him with more kindness over time until she and he became friends and she even apologized for hitting him with a ruler and brought him a small piece of cheese or fruit on occasion until he looked forward to talking with her.

Guido noticed she never did hit those who sat closest to her in winter anymore, and her God Given Beauty had disappeared.

When she did use the ruler again, which became very rare, it was so light it wouldn't break a young grape.

"Working In the Fields"

THE FIELDS

"You carry the small jug," Teodoro said as he handed the small brown and grey clay gallon jug of water with the oversized cork, which had been whittled down to fit, to little Guido.

Guido took the jug by the rope tied to the handle, carefully, remembering how he had dropped a jug once, but was lucky it dropped on grass in the field, and no one saw.

Papa had said, "I'll let you carry the water now, but big boys like you can't drop the jugs, they're expensive," and Guido was always careful not to let his father down, or to lose his slow march towards the jobs for the bigger boys on the farm.

Today, like the 5 days before, they would be working the "out field" some 3 miles from home.

Guido liked the walk there, and the slight hill of the land made it a little easier to break the soil, because you could pull the soil towards you with the hoe from higher to lower grade of land, and let gravity do the work.

Today they would prepare the soil to plant the lentils and chick peas.

He had explained the farm work to a 12-year-old girl who lived in town.

"We plant the orzo before winter. That's a rough grain to feed our mules and sell to people with horses. Potatoes, beans, chick peas, and lentils all plant in the spring, with potatoes going first in March, beans and peas in the beginning of April along with the garden vegetables."

Carmella, two years older than he, had a crush on little Guido and looked at him often during class, "I didn't know you knew so much about farming!"

Guido liked her. She always said nice things, and asked if he was going to be here or there a certain day, but Guido always said he'd be working on the farm because that was what they did every day, unless it was a holiday or wedding.

He didn't really understand girls...why they didn't want to work in the fields with the fresh air, but instead had to work by the hot ovens. He had seen his oldest brother wrestling with a girl in the barn, but she was letting him win, and his brother yelled at him, "Get out of here!"

"I have so many friends, and brothers, and my mamma and papa, I don't even know how I'd have time for a friend who is a girl," thought Guido.

"She likes you," Mamma had said as Guido saw a look in her eyes he'd not seen before.

These were the thoughts in Guido's mind as he placed the heavy piece of canvas cloth over his work boots, covering the toe, and wrapped the cloth around his ankle, securing it with a piece of light rope. Then the other foot, which was the way the boys kept the field dirt out of their shoes.

"Getting dirt in your shoes is a mistake you only make once," his papa had said.

Walking to the out field meant they'd have to carry all the tools they'd need, and water.

It was just dawn and they'd all had breakfast. Mamma had said goodbye and promised she'd bring Guido a piece of the yellow apple when she brought their lunch.

The boys walked along behind Teodoro, Guido walked beside Liberato (Leo), the quietest of the brothers. Liberato just walked and looked at the land, and Guido didn't think he'd stay a farmer.

"What do you want to be when you grow up?," Guido asked him.

"Something easier than farming," said Leo, slight of build with dark brown wavy hair, which some said resembled the look of a classical pianist.

They arrived at the field, and the boys made a line like a row of artillery in battle.

Guido had his own bedente, the tool used to work the soil. His papa made it with a bit shorter pole to fit Guido's height. The wood was smoothed like a modern hoe...a bit thicker at the end so you wouldn't lose your grip, with a two-pronged metal rake attached at the end, with flattened prongs to penetrate the soil easily.

The horizon was a soft grey blue and not a cloud in the sky, which meant good weather, although it didn't really matter too much about the weather because they'd have to work unless it was really pouring rain, and the brothers would even argue about that, as happened last week.

"It's raining," one had said.

"Not too much, we still can work," said Teodoro.

"No, no it's a hard rain, let's walk home."

Guido just listened. He wasn't old enough to say whether they'd work, or where, but he could say he was tired and needed a rest, or to pee, or wanted something to drink.

The boys' hands were hard with calluses from years of working the soil.

To open the soil for spring planting, you swing the bedente up over your head, letting the weight carry it, and let it "plop" into the soil, but not too deeply into the soil today, because it wasn't corn, just lentils.

They'd start in a line at the bottom of the hill and work their way up, then go back down to a new line.

This way, when you pulled the soil, it would fall down the hill from gravity.

Not all did the work with equal enthusiasm.

Frank was fastest, and was often hired by local farmers for his speed, but he didn't work all the soil then, but instead simply pushed crumbled soil from above onto the row of soil below, leaving every other row untilled. From a distance it looked the same, but fields he worked would yield less.

"I wonder why they all say Frank is the best when he doesn't work *all* the soil. Did they not notice?" All they'd say was, "Frank is fastest," and look at the others with a frown.

The talk in the fields was quick, a little of this, a little of that, but not much, because it was hard work and you were breathing hard.

Guido didn't mind the first half of the day because your muscles weren't too tired, and you had lunch brought by Mamma or one of the girls to look forward to.

The later in the day, the harder the work, as you were tired and your muscles ached, and there was the unrelenting sun and sweat and soil on your skin.

He'd get bored, and try to think of something else, but you had to be careful because you could get hurt if you didn't keep your mind on your work, like the boy who hit his brother's toe with a bedente, and the injured brother had left to work in the city.

Weeds would be piled in little mounds, but the stones were a real problem. They'd have to get the mule and drag the stone out of the field, which wasted a lot of time, and Papa would look down and say, "Things are too slow."

Today was a good day because a bedente had broken and Guido was chosen to walk home to get a replacement. His small feet walked on the raised humps of dirt on the path churned by the cart's wheels in a rain. He would walk on the tops until they would crumble and then he'd hop up on top of the ridge again.

He saw the crows flying and spread his arms to pretend he was a bird, free to fly all over the world and oceans, and see sheiks in Arabia, and looked in the pond to see if he could find a frog in the low part, but couldn't find one fast, so skipped along home.

On a good day of work Papa would say, "How much you've done!," and Guido would be happy.

Guido had overheard his father explaining to Liberato, "We only have 20 acres, and we don't own that, so half the yield goes to the land-owner. I want you boys to stay here, but if you can find a better way, I understand."

"Separating the Wheat from the Chaff"

A HARVEST

The soil had been turned, by hand or by mule, depending on the lay of the land.

The wheat had been planted, and weeded, and cared for, and Guido rose knowing his favorite part would come today...separating the wheat from the chaff.

First, just after sunup, they'd prepare the flat circular clay area of ground 30 feet across, specially set aside for just this task.

After a breakfast of apples, oatmeal and cheese, Guido ran from the cistern to the circle of clay, with bucket after bucket of water.

He'd run and throw the bucket of water into the air, see the sparkling droplets sweep to the sky and land on the grey-toned clay with a "slop" sound, as his brothers armed with long brooms swept the water over the clay.

Wherever the water landed, the clay would turn a darker grey, with each sweep of the broom a gigantic brushstroke, fading quickly in the sun and heat.

Again and again the water droplets rose to the sky, again and again the brush would swish, and Guido would see the lovely patterns, see them fade, then run for more water.

Heavy baskets of wheat were rolled onto the clay slab and dumped one by one until there was a huge mound which they'd spread with pitchforks and wooden rakes.

Next came the huge four foot wide, circular flat stone, five inches thick with a hole through it, near the edge, where the chain went through which was tied to a rope.

This was attached to a donkey, mule, or cow, and by leading the animal just so, you controlled the path of the stone.

The gentle working of the stone against the clay floor loosened the chaff from the wheat. The work went on for hours, circle after circle.

After lunch, when the wind was just above a whisper, they all took wooden shovels and threw the mix of grain and chaff into the air.

The light wind caught the yellow chaff and these speckles slowly fell to the ground outside the circle, leaving whole wheat kernels on the clay slab.

Guido always enjoyed the sweet smell of the chaff and the crunching sounds of grain under his bare feet.

Sometimes the chaff would look like mountains made of fluff, and the kernels like a desert. Stretching his arms out, he would pretend he was a plane and was looking out the window to see his desert below. He turned his feet as he walked in the kernel berries, and heard them crunch, rolling one against the other.

Guido thought this a perfect time to tell the joke he'd learned at school, and if it went well with his brothers, he'd tell Mamma and Papa tonight.

"A man is getting paid to cut down a forest, and the first day he cuts down 15 trees. 'Ohh, I am making good progress and will be done in just a few days.' But the second day, he only cuts down 12, the next day, 8. 'What am I doing wrong?,' he asked the man on the donkey."

"You worked hard each day?"

"Yes."

"Hmmm…but did you take time to sharpen your axe?"

His brothers groaned and said, "Guido this is not a joke, it's stupid."

"No, no, it's funny, it is!"

He liked it because the man didn't see that he should have sharpened the axe. That's what made it funny!

"Don't you see, he worked so hard and cut less and less and all he had to do was sharpen his axe! It doesn't cost anything to sharpen the axe! See how funny he is!"

He laughed thinking about the man and how silly he was. He would tell it to Mamma and Papa anyway, they might like it better, and his brothers might have refused to laugh just to play a joke on him.

After their meal which Mamma brought out to them so they wouldn't make a mess in the house, "Too much dust, don't bring it in here!," the grains were scooped with wooden shovels into burlap bags and tied with rope.

The owner of the land came as they were filling the sacks and Papa told them to speed up a little as the man had to get home to his dinner.

All the sacks were put in the middle of the slab, then the land owner took half which the boys would load into his wagon.

Guido was proud when he saw all the sacks of grain in the center of the clay circle, and remembered all the work in preparing the soil and the smell of the land, the many hours spent weeding and removing rocks, the clay slab and water and brushes.

And then it hit him. It wasn't that he was angry, it just seemed unfair.

"All our work for this? It's a good yield of sacks, but when the land-owner took half," he thought, "all that work for just half?"

At dinner, Guido said what he'd been thinking, "Why should he take half, he didn't do any of the work?"

"He owns the land, it's his land."

What he thought next he did not say to his mamma and papa, and brothers, because he thought it would hurt their feelings.

Thinking to himself he said, "This is a stupid deal. He takes too much. He does no work, but takes so much of the yield."

From that day forward, he was thinking of a way he could do better.

One day, Grandma was sitting on the porch peeling apples. Guido told her what he'd been thinking, and how bad it was they had so little left, and how the man took the sacks but didn't work, and then he said it, "It's a stupid deal, we keep too little. I will find a better way when I'm bigger."

She said nothing, but patted his head and held his face in her hands, "You were always the smart one."

THEIR OWN TV SHOW

The three boys (Guido, Domenico, and Vittorio), stuck their dark straight-haired heads around the front door of Vittorio's father's bar, which was just a poorly lit room attached to the house.

Vittorio's father had told them, "You're not old enough to come in the bar, don't you come in here without my say so."

Men dusty and tired from a day of farming in Fossalto would find their way there and tell stories of pigs, and plows, and crops. It didn't make much money but Vittorio's father enjoyed people, and preferred the rumblings of men to women's talk, having grown up in a family of eight boys.

Most important, it was the only place in town with a television.

"Guido, my papa said we're not supposed to go in the bar," said Vittorio, 4 years younger than Guido, as all three peered at the TV screen.

Guido said sharply, "We're not in the bar, we're out here. We're allowed to be out here."

The boys were watching their favorite show, a comedy with three performers; a tall slender silly girl named Delia Scalla, the tall comedian Nino Man Fredi, and the straight man-and slightly slow, Paolo Panelli.

Guido spent months explaining how they could put together their own similar comedy act.

"But Guido, we don't have a TV station."

"You're crazy. They didn't either in the beginning, they just had a comedy group and we can have one too. I'll be Nino Man Fredi, Domenico

(Guido's second cousin) can be Paolo Panelli, and you get to be the best role, Delia Scalla."

"She's a girl, there's no way I'm gonna be a girl!," said Vittorio.

"No, you don't understand. You're not a girl. Everybody knows you're who you are...they know you're a man (and Guido said this to appeal to Vittorio's sense of manhood, since he was small and often called a girl by kids), and you're the best actor, and this will be hardest role."

"Believe me," said Guido, "everybody is going to laugh most at what *you* do, and we'll dress you up so it's like making fun. Nobody will think it's anything but hilarious."

Guido looked at Vittorio, but he just stared at the ground, "I'm not going to be the girl."

"Look, I'll bet you Pierina (the girl Vittorio had a crush on in school, but would not even look his way in class), will like you when she hears how funny you are in the role. She's gonna talk to you and give you a kiss. I'll bet you, I'll bet you she does that."

Finally Guido had found the golden note, the idea that would make things happen, as his grandmother had explained to him. "Everybody has their own ideas, you gotta look at life from their way," she'd said.

And so it was that the comedy troupe was formed. In a town of few, of farmers, they quickly became a hit, and soon were asked to every pig slaughter party in the town.

They'd get free food and be able to dance all night with the pretty girls. Vittorio had forgotten about the girl in school and was dancing with all the girls whenever they performed.

And in fact, the audience loved Vittorio best because he was a very good girl and kept hamming it up more and more, until Domenico thought Vittorio was becoming the star, but Guido said, "If you don't want to be the girl, Domenico, then keep your mouth quiet. He's funny, everybody thinks he's funny, it's OK."

"I'm going to butcher a pig next Sunday," Mr. Willionce said to Guido on the street, "and you boys are going to have to be there. We laughed so hard last week my wife peed herself, so she says you gotta come but she's gonna use the toilet before you start."

It started in the morning about ten o'clock. About 15 people were there to start. They boiled the water, and a boy went to get the pig from the barn. The meat would feed the family for about four months, and there'd be plenty for all to eat at the party.

The little boy brought the pig from the barn, and Guido's father took the sharp hook with the handle and lanced the pig just under the chin.

Then six men hoisted the pig up on the table, and Guido's father sliced the veins by the neck, and the blood rushed out in torrents into the large bucket. "You should'a been a surgeon," the one farmer said.

They hung the pig by its feet for about an hour, and then the women took the blood into the kitchen and put it on the stove, stirring until it became the consistency of heavy cream. Then it was poured into pans to cool, to be eaten over the months ahead with salt and orange peel, a delicacy.

One by one, or by twos, more people from Fossalto came. Guido and his troupe were treated like royalty.

"Are you boys ready to perform?"

"No, we don't start till 8 tonight, but we're gonna eat the pig till then!"

The men and women would touch their arms as they passed them, or pat their heads and laugh, and the young girls stared at Vittorio.

"He is sooo funny, how can he do that?," said the girl from the farm by the Valley.

"Everybody loves him and thinks he's funny, Dorina peed herself last week when they performed, so we had to come. Papa says he'll own the bar someday," Torina said.

Giovanni the accordionist arrived about six o'clock with his brother who played violin, and they ate pig and wine and bread with all the guests till around seven, when the owner glanced at Guido, and then a nod.

The boys always liked to have about an hour to get dressed and "prepare" as Guido had explained. "Look, we have to be special. So, an hour before we perform, we go to a room in the house, and leave the door open, and people will see us but know we're special, and then when we come out they will clap."

Guido's friend took the wooden microphone with the wire attached, (it was no microphone, just a prop Guido made in his barn), and put it in the room.

Then, it was time.

Someone yelled, "Quiet please, the show is to begin," and the looks on the faces of the guests returned to that of their youth...expectant, and eager for fun.

The three boys walked out confidently and took their places, and everybody grabbed a few more pieces of food and wine, running to sit down quickly.

The skit tonight was about a girl who pretended to like one boy, and then the other, and then got mixed up in her lies about who she liked better, the two men arguing about what she'd said, then challenging each other to a duel of throwing rags at each other to the death, while she screams and pleads with them to stop.

They all end up in a heap, with the girl just deciding to be friends with both, because, "Love is too difficult for my sensitive nature."

It was a *"bit"* Guido had made up and it was one of the crowd's favorites, because everybody there could throw their napkin or a rag, and the laughter would last for 20 minutes.

Pierina caught Vittorio later that night when he and Guido were outside the house. She threw her arms around him and said he was the funniest woman she'd ever met and gave him a kiss that started on his cheek like his mother gave him, but she slowly slid her lips over his cheek to his mouth and gave him a long kiss as she stroked his back with her fingers.

The next day, Vittorio said to Guido, "You were right, Guido, you we're right!"

15 WITH TYPHOID FEVER

Dr. Pompilio Cornacchione was a rotund, bald doctor, who always stammered "ahem," when he spoke.

The doctor would always come to the home of a sick child, but only by horse, so Guido's father rode a borrowed horse to the doctor's home, which the doctor rode to the farm while Guido's father stayed at the doctor's office.

The trip to Fossalto to see Guido took an entire day, and cost the family three days income.

Guido's mother could barely hear the doctor's words in the next room.

"Ahem, you have a fever, Guido. How long have you been having this fever?," said the doctor as he pushed his hands over Guido's abdomen, his hands feeling the inflamed and slightly distended lower right side of Guido's abdomen.

"Guido, how long have you had the fever?"

His mother stood by the door. She spoke, "He's had the fever for nine days, we told you."

Guido's eyes were milky and wet, his black hair pasted to his sweating forehead, and to him, the scene was like a dream.

He could see everything clearly; saw the doctor and his mother, and could feel his own body, the extreme fatigue and soreness on his butt from days of wet diarrhea, but when he tried to move it was like a day's work.

Again the doctor asked, "Guido, how long have you had the fever?"

"Huh?"

Guido began to concentrate, *"now what did the doctor ask? Oh yes, he asked how long..."*

"In the fields all day, we work all day." Then realizing the question was not about the length of the workday, but something else, he opened his mouth to speak but forgot the words. "Now, what was how long?," he asked himself. He knew he could remember if he tried and he looked out at the sky and saw the little dazzling specs that sometimes slide over your eyes, and he thought it was like a light snow...

The doctor sat with his hands crossed on the bed with Guido, saying to Guido's mother, "Ahem, I'm not going to lie to you, I think I know what he has and I'm not often wrong on these things, but I suppose it is possible I could be wrong this time, but I don't think so," he said in a slow monotone voice as he sipped the homemade dolce or sweet wine.

It reminded him of his own mother's sweet wine which she served in a white china decanter... "How lucky they are to live this good life in the country while I travel to and fro everyday and half the time get no pay," he thought.

He looked directly into the eyes of Guido's mother, knowing they always loved their children most, and hated to hear bad news, but hated even more to be told a lie.

And he knew she would have the strength, push come to shove, to hear the words, and he really did hope he would not have to view a small boy's casket once again because above all things, he hated early death in a family- especially in a farm family, where every pair of hands was the only insurance against starvation and failure.

"Salmonella typhi is transmitted by ingesting food or water from another infected person, the bacteria perforating through the intestinal wall, characterized by a slowly progressing fever which can be as high as 104 degrees," he said as he remembered the pride his father had in his ability to memorize pathology in medical school.

"What did you say, I'm not clear about that?," said Mamma.

"It's typhoid fever, and the prognosis is not good. He may not live, but he has about 2 chances in 3 of surviving."

In modern times, a strong dose of a full-spectrum antibiotic such as ciprofloxacin would knock the flagellated bacterium right out of the body in two days, but in those times, in the time Guido was ill, the disease ravaged the body at will, and you lived or died, depending on the whim of what the farmer's called "the grim reaper."

"You will have to do as I tell you in the care of your son," the doctor said as he outlined what little could be done.

"Let me pay you over time," said Mamma, and the doctor nodded. "Of course," he said as a jug of dolce (sweet) wine was placed in the pack on the horse that would take him back to town.

Morning after morning, day after day, evening after evening, his mother prepared the little pastinas in broth with a bit of wine. It was like watering a plant. If the food was too thick, the diarrhea would start again, with the chills and fever and wet bedding. But just the right amount of liquid and pastina, and Guido could keep it down, and the fever subside.

The fever left first, then very slowly the rose-colored patches on his skin began to return to normal. His parents had told him he had food poisoning, and he wondered what he had eaten. "It was the goat from the party a month ago, I will never eat goat again. I should have known better." He would tell his mother over and over about the goat and she would say, "Yes, Guido. I'm sure you are right, no more goat," and look

at him for a long time, not looking anywhere but at his face while stroking his hands.

Day after day was the same. When alone, he'd say, "I will lift my legs
over the bed, then I can walk to the kitchen."

He'd struggle to lift his legs, but just sitting up felt like an entire day's work.
There was no energy to stand, and then he'd slump back to the bed again.

After seven weeks he could sit up, then by the eighth week, he learned
to walk again, groping his hands at the walls to hold up his weight, falling, raising up and falling again.

Then he could walk to the outhouse and he never thought he'd be so
glad to be there again.

And then he could walk.

"When will Guido work in the fields with us again, Papa?," said one
of his brothers.

"Guido will not go to the fields anymore, he'll work by the house so
he can lie down if he needs to."

"But that's not fair. We're supposed to share the easier work by the
house, every seventh day, every one of us."

And Guido's life changed. It seemed that everyone was always concerned with his health, even when he felt fine.

True, he'd lost weight and never really gained it all back, but he *could*
work and he fed the cows each morning, and sensed the unfairness his
brothers felt, but never said to his face.

It was difficult...he felt others viewed him as an invalid, but he knew
he was well.

But he had lived, being on the better side of two out of three.

A FIRST STEP AWAY

It had been a hard decision for Guido. "There's nothing for you here Guido, go do something better," his mother had told him adding, "I will make you leave if you don't go on your own. You can do better," she said as she wiped her tears and hugged him.

What he did not tell his mother was that he had to go because he did not want to be perceived as an invalid. "I am as strong as anyone else. I'm well, I know I am, and I can do any of the same work anyone else can."

But he said nothing of this, because he knew that the decision had been made by his parents. The easier work he received on the farm came at the cost of his brothers having to work harder in the fields. But the silence on the topic just made it seem bigger and bigger in his mind.

A relative had taken a job in a larger city caring for a family's home, and because she lived with the family, she was able to save money.

"Can you find something like that for me on a farm?," he asked her. At 19 he was looking more at girls, but was not interested in this girl because she had not worked hard in school and was rude to her grandmother.

The job which she found for Guido was in Bagnacavallo, a city of 30,000 people, ten times larger than Fossalto, and the farm was fully mechanized with tractors and pesticides and fertilizers.

An odd conversation had occurred with his father, "You will see things in the big city you won't like, Guido. I lived in a big city once… (silence)…but you will learn for yourself. I wish you the best and hope your dreams for a better life come true," his father said as he hugged him a long time.

Guido moved to Bagnacavallo and lived with a wife and husband and two kids.

Each night he would play with the children by the fire. He would push the wooden trucks on the rough wooden floor with the boy, and hold the little girl's doll. They called him their "little Guido."

And at night, he would lie in bed thinking of home and the fields, and his brothers and parents, and for the first time had his own room.

Guido saw that their apples, pears and grapes *were* bigger and *looked* better, but lacked the pungent, rich taste of the foods from his village where fruits were grown using the old ways like at home.

This farm grew wheat and grapes for wine, apples and pears, cherries and olives.

On his home farm, if an apple had a worm, they threw it aside, here everything was sprayed.

The local farmers knew that modern farming produced more food with less taste, but for the city folks, size and color seemed all that mattered.

City folks just didn't seem to understand quality.

Guido overheard the son of the owner with a wholesale buyer.

"These apples, they don't taste so good," said the buyer.

"Look how big they are, and red, and when you put them on the shelf the customers will buy them all. Everything we grow sells...and at top dollar. See how big, see how red, and nice and juicy!"

He had been honest, the apples were big and red, and nice and juicy, but they also *really didn't* have much taste.

Apple and pear trees lived only as long as they gave maximum yield, and then were cut down and another planted in its place. (Older trees produce less, but the fruit has a much stronger and better taste.)

The grapes were run on wires between trees along the dirt road, to make spraying easier. Between the trees were planted broccoli and lettuce.

Where Guido once had strolled on his father's land in Fossalto, now he drove a truck with a drum and chemicals on back, spraying.

They ate breakfast together, then Guido fed the animals and worked the fields, then back at noon for pasta or meat.

They traveled by tractor, to save time.

When it was time to eat, the farm bell rang, like a factory.

He saved about $10 a month, and knew quickly he didn't want to stay.

Guido remembered a conversation he'd had with his father, reflecting another view on farming. "We should let the vines grow bigger, they'll make more wine which we can sell to the people of Fossalto," said Guido.

"No," his father said "Our vines are for our own wine. We produce fewer, small grapes, but they taste better."

One day, Guido confronted the owner's son of the farm where he worked.

"Why do we grow the big red apples when the little ones taste better?"

"Look, you came from a small town where everybody knows farming. The customers don't know the difference."

"They go into the store and pick out the biggest apple, or the one without spots, so they think it's better. What's important Guido is it's what they buy, the big shiny one. It's not the taste, it's the big shiny apple, and we get our money and making money is what it's all about. Why do you look shocked?"

Asked Guido, "Would you want to eat them?"

"I eat them, but we get our apples from the small farmers around here."

"Why?"

"They taste better."

TO GREAT BRITAIN AND MEETING THE BEATLES, PART I

It was about six o'clock in the evening, and the sky filled with soft red stripes and the air hung heavy with humidity. Guido walked the streets of Bagnacavallo, the small town near the farm where he worked. It reminded him of his own home in Fossalto. Not that it looked like home, it didn't, but more that he was surrounded by families as he walked the streets.

He peered in one window after another, and he felt that somehow, for the first time in his life, he was living in a world without a true home. In one window, he saw a family at dinner, the bearded patriarch at the head cutting the pig with a gigantic knife, his wife and daughters laughing and lifting their wine glasses and toasting to something he could not hear, and the two grandparents bent forward in their wheelchairs like two birds on a wire. The little girl clutched her doll, shiny black button eyes, pulling the dress just so, and scolding the doll for some imagined wrongdoing.

In another window down the street of offset stucco homes with their red tile roofs and stains on the outer walls, left from years of rainwater dripping, he could see three women bringing bread out of the oven on a wooden paddle, dark from years of use.

The smell wafted through the air like a current of rushing water before him. He entered it, and then was in it, and the current took him back in his mind to his mother's own bread and oven, and the small doll shaped breads she would make for his sisters and their squeals of happiness as they pulled the arms apart and ate them, spilling crumbs on the floor which his mother picked up laughing.

So many times it is a small seemingly insignificant twist of fate that determines the lot of men and women in this life.

Such was the case when he picked up an opened newspaper from the street and peered at it prior to dropping it into the trash.

"Wanted....Experienced Chef for Brighton England Restaurant, people of Italian descent preferred."

It was a beachside resort in Brighton, England, across the Channel from France, and the job was for only six to seven months, March to September of the year.

And so, for some reason, not really from any rational consideration supported by logic or fed by a young man's considerations, he tore out the ad, jammed it in his back pocket, and later that night pulled it out with the intention of throwing it away. But instead, flattened it with his fingers on the wooden writing desk.

To his own surprise (as much as anyone's had they seen him that night at his writing desk) he picked up the pen, dipped it in the dark blue ink and filled out the job application, listing every top restaurant he'd ever heard of in Rome in the column marked, "experience."

"I just wanted to see what they were going to say."

Two weeks later he was working in the fields, pruning the grapevines and singing a tune from his hometown named Che La Luna, when the field bell rang out.

"It's not even noon, why are they ringing the bell?"

The mailman had part of his leg shot off in one of the desperate routs of the Germans by Russian forces in World War II in Poland, and his wooden peg leg rested on the pedal of his bicycle.

"Guido, this is for you from England, from a restaurant. What do you want with England? Their food is terrible, even the English don't want to eat it."

He signed for the letter and went into his room in the house. The brown envelope tore open easily.

"Your application as Chef has been approved. You are directed to report to Milano for a physical. A train ticket is enclosed." He stared at the ticket for some time, and thought of returning it. It never really dawned on him he'd get the job.

Later that night Guido walked to the café and met his close friend, Antonio, a tall, dark, skinny young man of 20 with a slight scar on his chin, which he claimed came from a fight, but his sister said he fell on a plow.

"Are you going to go?" asked Antonio. "You know nothing of cooking. Tell me the truth, have you ever cooked anything at all at any time in your life?"

"Ever cooked even part of a meal, anything, anything at all? Ok then, have you ever even held a kitchen pot in your hand? Warmed something up perhaps?"

Guido searched his memory and found that in fact he had never cooked anything in his entire life. His mother and sisters did all the cooking, and in the field his brother did the cooking, and here the family did the cooking, and he hadn't even lifted a skillet once to his memory.

"I watched them cook," said Guido.

"Are you going to lie and say you can cook?," said his red-haired, light-skinned friend, Georgio (the banker's son) over a beer the next day.

"I won't lie, but I'll bet you a case of beer I'll take the job."

"Ok, Guido, we'll bet a case of beer."

"Let me see you have the money," said Guido.

"We have the money. If you lose, you buy the beer so let's see your money."

"Meeting The Beatles"

TO GREAT BRITAIN AND MEETING
THE BEATLES, PART II

The Brighton restaurant owner, himself Italian, was a portly man and short, with dark happy eyes and fat short fingers with perfectly manicured fingernails with a coat of clear nail polish.

It struck Guido immediately that his laughter preceded every phrase he spoke. "So, ha ha ha, you come from Fossalto? Good! Italian people, all my cooks are Italians," he said as his fat finger pointed to the restaurant.

The cooks worked ten hours a day, got free food and slept in simple white-walled apartments above.

"You can have steak twice a week, other days you eat fish or chicken, and one beer a day. You trust me, I trust you," he said tapping Guido's chest with his finger.

Guido of course had never cooked anything in his entire life, "You show me how you want the food prepared and I'll do it your way."

The staff was so universally sick of prima donnas who came from the country boasting of every conceivable accomplishment, half of it made up, be it how many acres they could weed in a day, their cooking skills and talent, or exploits of love, that not one employee ever asked him about his early jobs in food service.

("God gave you two ears, but one mouth, so you think that through," his grandmother had told him on the porch.)

The restaurant was along a busy pedestrian-traveled street in a tourist town, one block from the waterfront, a mix of brownstone buildings and rushing traffic and a huge clock tower in the center of town, visible from the restaurant, which chimed every quarter hour.

Street vendors in drab brown and grey with missing front teeth sold their fish and chips, the oily smell blowing in lightly-colored blue smoke plumes every day, and sitting like smog on windless days.

The flow of world travelers was unending. Blondes from Sweden, dark-haired beauties from Italy, the British girls, and a torrent of students on holiday. The preferred date was *always* an Italian man because they would listen and touch you gently, appropriately.

Large glass windows in the front of the restaurant revealed a cacophony of images and sounds, almost surreal, something like what you might see in a Norman Rockwell painting.

Table after table jammed close with customers bumping customers as they ate.

And in the center of the restaurant, like a small ship in a frothing sea, a long table where Guido and the other cooks prepared steak and French fries and peas the British took for good food, but which Guido never liked much.

In the back of the restaurant was another cooking station, then a wall, with windows through which the prep cooks could view the customers.

Through that window when carrying a stainless steel tray of beef, Guido saw her; Rina, with her dark flowing luscious hair, rich tan skin, and natural athleticism.

He was attracted to her immediately, and she smiled back when he peered at her through the kitchen window.

"How do you like the food, is everything OK?," he asked when she appeared near his window.

"Yes, yes, everything's fine."

He met her at 8:00 that night under the bell tower. She talked for over an hour of her home town and the man she was to marry, selected by her parents because his family owned a factory.

He stared at her lips, beautifully shaped, expressive, and he longed to kiss her when her shoulder touched his lightly as they walked.

"I know she cares for me but she's only marrying him because his family is rich," he shared with a friend the next day.

"Let me tell you something, farm boy. You can love her all you want, but she's going to go for that factory kid for the dough. That's the way it is, but you can waste all the time in the world with her. Waste away, while the world of beauties sits in front of you," he said his hands outstretched to the young women in the restaurant.

Guido felt that her heart was his. He *knew*. The way she looked at him and the long hugs when they parted, and the kisses on his cheek.

He'd lay in bed at night dreaming of meeting her parents; "This is Guido, who worked hard with his family every day on the farm, an honest man, and see he's now in Brighton with all the world ahead of him," and, "I know he's poor, but they love each other and he has character."

"Yes, character," said the Grandmother, who looked so much like his own, with her knitting and knowing eyes.

And she'd marry him and wear a white wedding gown, and his brother would tie a cow bell under the bed and it would clank all night that first night, and they'd have beautiful kids.

Every time he saw her his dreams awoke anew. Every hint of her unhappiness with the arranged marriage was a sign she was ready to love him, that she cared for him, that she wanted to be his.

"I'm going home next week and I'm going to marry the factory owner's son, Goodbye Guido."

Not even a hug or a kiss, she just walked away.

That night he went to the bar across the street and four musicians sat with him.

"So you guys play music?"

"Yeah," said John. "We play up and down all along here."

Their hair was long and they wore rough clothing with black leather, and had their own ways in things.

"What's the name of your band?"

"We call ourselves the Beatles, but we're thinking of changing our name," said Paul.

Many times in the years ahead he thought of the meeting with the Beatles and how something small can become so big in time, and of Rina.

"Little Vincenza at Her Bread Table"

LITTLE VINCENZA

Little Vincenza stood dutifully by her mother, Nunzia, in her blue and white dress with the canvas apron which tied behind her waist, mixing the dough just as her mother had told her, in her own little table made for her by Papa.

It was shorter than that used by adults, sanded unvarnished oak all held together with wooden pins, and just the right height for her to easily reach down and knead the bread, which she did each morning before school.

She was very proud of her table. It had a working area of 5 feet by 2 feet, with angled-out sides coming up about 8 inches all around. It was hers, and forever an indication that she had arrived at a job of real importance to the family.

And next to the table, on a stool made by Papa was her doll Papin, a foot high with a porcelain face, and no child was more gingerly cared for and primped.

Vincenza pretended Papin could talk, and each step of the kneading was done with the whispered guidance of the doll. "Papin says to lay the dough in a glob on the table," said Vincenza, "Papin says to push the sides into the middle, but slowly, not quickly."

Her mother watched the antics and laughed quietly, but never so Vincenza could hear her, as Vincenza's care for the doll Papin was exceeded only in life by Nunzia's daily care and oversight of her daughter.

Vincenza clearly remembered the day her mother had asked her husband, Alfio Ciraldo, a Sicilian whose entire life was spent in 80 degrees and sunshine, to make it.

Like many a wise wife, she navigated his Sicilian temper with the deftness of a captain of a sailing ship in the swirling Magellan Straights near Cape Horn, asking things only after he'd had his favorite meal of prosciutto, his favorite dolce wine, and perhaps after a night of love making.

"Alfio, today you will have time to make her a little bread table?"

"What, this is crazy! Put her on a stool, she won't fall," but he *knew* he would make the table in the end.

"No, no," said his wife, "She likes things you make, and you make such nice pieces. She wants one too, and I can't tell her no."

"Well, it will only take an hour or so," he said as she took out the ingredients of his favorite meal, glancing to him with eyes that said she was willing.

And each morning as the mother and daughter mixed the dough, enough for 12 loaves, Nunzia would secretly reach into her apron and plop a chocolate covered almond into her daughter's mouth, then one in her own mouth.

"Good little girls get the best treats!," she said and it was no surprise to those who saw the daughter and mother together, that as Vincenza grew up, her favorite use of time was to be with her mother, making those quiet times in life fun.

COMING TO AMERICA

Guido sat in the center isle of the 707 jet for the 8 hour flight from England to the United States, drinking what would with kindness be described as a moderate quality wine in his home town.

He truly believed this was the worst glass of red wine he'd ever tasted. It looked like red wine and smelled like red wine, but the flavor was hard and lifeless, and with each sip his mind hoped to taste the wine of his father's...a hope that rose and fell with each sip.

"My friend Vittorio's father threw away an entire barrel of wine better than this," he said under his breath, remembering that its taste was like vinegar, but overall, really somewhat better than this.

There was no place to throw it, so his mind diverted to a game he'd enjoyed since childhood...glancing politely from passenger to passenger, trying to decide which country each person on the plane came from.

"The long blonde-haired, slender woman in her early twenties doted on an older man, likely her father. Maybe Sweden?"

"The dark-skinned man in the custom made suit two isles up? Certainly an Italian, who else would invest in a fine suit of clothes."

His breathing slowed, and hand fell a few inches, until a flight attendant with trim blue cap and white piping gently pried the glass from his hand and placed it in the white plastic trash bag.

In his light sleep his mind's eye remembered the events of the last year leading to his trip to America.

His brother Frank's letter was short, "It's fall and things will be slow in wintertime at the restaurant in Brighton, England, so come to visit me in Barberton, Ohio, and don't say no Guido because I'm older than you. You will find there are more opportunities here."

Guido knew he could not enter the U.S. and get a Visa without a letter guaranteeing that his employer at the restaurant in England had a job waiting for him upon his return.

"I will only be gone for a few months, just to visit my brother, Frank," said Guido.

"Now you're not going to run off on me are you Guido? You don't have a girl in the U.S.? A long pause which Guido knew was the owner's way, then "Only stay 3 months, then come back to me and we'll make more money...and we'll find a girl here for you, maybe an English girl."

The U.S. customs office at the point of entry in New York was drab, with harsh overhead lights, and bright white walls with no art of any kind. Only a sole calendar with hash marks over days elapsed decorated the room, and even it was a-kilter. The officer was drab and his questions were drab.

"Why did you have a piece of lemon in the napkin in your suit?"

"I told you, I felt sick on the plane and the stewardess, she gave it to me."

The official sat staring at the slice of lemon on the table, twirling it with his index finger, and staring at Guido as his mind covered all the possible explanations for the lemon...to see if it might signify some reason to reject this skinny Italian.

"What is this letter?"

"This is a letter from my brother, Frank, I told you."

"Don't get smart, read it to me!"

"I'm not going to read it to you, I refuse. It's from my brother. It's none of your business."

The official decided that a criminal would not cross him and that in fact Guido was just a country boy.

"Now look, don't get smart in America. You should be respectful," he said as he pushed the lemon and letter back at Guido."

"Approved!," he said as Guido pocketed the letter and put the lemon and napkin back in his pocket."

AMERICA THE BEAUTIFUL

At first glance, to be frank, America did not impress.

At least not the America he saw from the plane as it prepared to land in Cleveland, Ohio.

The houses around the airport were jammed so close together they looked like sugar cubes lined in a row, and where was their land to grow vegetables?

Roads with white snow topped with dark grit, it looked like a black and white photograph of ice cream with grey and black sprinkles.

He was amazed at the huge double-wheeled trucks with the blades on front pushing snow right off the roads, the number of cars, the new condition of cars- in so many styles, and the stores where the amount of merchandise for sale, always On Sale, was beyond what anyone in Italy could dream of in their wildest fantasies.

It was super-market, and super-go, and super-sized, and the whole idea of *super* mesmerized him.

But the tantalizing goods and material wealth were not what fascinated him, held him entranced, and made him *sure* he would do whatever he had to do to stay in America. It was something else, something which struck deep in the heart of a boy from a family farm in Fossalto.

In Italy, if you come from a wealthy family, then doors open. You have a future.

You go to college, get a degree, and when you go to the bank, the teller waves you to the front of the line and compliments your new suit and tie.

But as a poor farmer's son, not so.

He remembered the time his father removed his cap in town and bowed his head to say hello to a lawyer and doctor walking by. The two didn't even nod.

"Why do you say hello to them if they don't say hello to you?," Guido asked his Father.

"Someday, I may need their help, and they see me...they just didn't let you know."

Guido thought to himself, "Why would they not let me know?," but he kept walking quietly beside his father.

This was the very first time that Guido realized his papa might say something which, while not entirely true, would protect Guido's or another person's feelings, or their pride.

But here, in America, people with power and money were pretty much the same as everyone else, courteous and friendly, even the lawyers and doctors.

They'd smile and say hello when they passed, or even stop to talk.

"Perhaps because anyone can become rich if they work hard and long enough?," he thought.

"This is a place where a farmer's son can become something. Where I could be somebody and make a good life, not scratching on a farm to give the landowner half the grain."

In that moment, Guido knew he was not likely to leave America, and perhaps should give some thought to what kind of woman he wanted for a wife and to have children with.

A CHOICE OF CAREER...
HAIR STYLIST

It had perplexed Guido for many years...exactly what *did* he want to do with his life?

Like many who have multiple talents and a strong work ethic, the choice was made more difficult by the sheer number of possibilities open to him.

After all, he was in America in its booming post World War II years, and there was a sense that anything could be done.

He had excelled at farming and done well as a cook, but beyond that the world seemed like an ocean of unlimited size and endless possibilities, like the perplexed mindset one struggles with when faced with 40 flavors of ice cream.

The more there are to pick from, the harder it is to pick.

Guido, like so many other people in life, was to learn the ringing truth in the words, "timing is everything."

Donato, like Guido, had grown up in Fossalto, Italy, working on a farm, and had come to this country about the same time as Guido's brother, Frank.

With perfect teeth, a stocky build and straight light brown hair which hung down near his shoulders in a style that could only be interpreted as European.

But the thing people noticed most, and women revered and loved most about Donato was his genuine interest in all people and uncanny ability to remember every name, every story, and every fact to pass his path in life.

It amazed everyone. He could remember any name from his entire lifetime from just one meeting, and beyond this, the ins and outs and details of every story and secret shared, so that seeing him again after years had passed he could say, "How is your mother, Maria, and are you still making the dolce wine?," and then giggle with his high-pitched laugh which cut through the air like a crystal knife.

All like it had happened yesterday.

People felt important around him, and sought his company, liked him, and his seven-year-old hair styling business in America was doing a brisk business, and growing.

Donato visited Guido's brother Frank's home often- a dark red brick, simple home in Barberton, as they laughed over memories of Fossalto, Italy, amidst the smells of fresh-baked bread made by Carmela, Frank's wife, tasting each others' homemade wine with only polite criticisms, and spoke of the same things in the same way.

They found in each others' company that one unifying balm to mankind worldwide, the oasis of that which is familiar.

"Guido, I'm going down to the beauty school in Akron. I need to find a new assistant. Why don't you come with me and check it out?," said Donato.

Dr. Gerber, the owner of Gerber's Beauty School, walked to greet Donato inside the school. Donato was one of his prize students, making money, and most important, hiring his students.

"This is my cousin Guido. (Any Italian from Fossalto qualified as family here in America.) Unless he finds a beautiful girl to marry, he's gonna have to go home."

Dr. Gerber was 5 ft. 10, slim with blondish hair, immaculately dressed, and walked with steps covering twice the normal man's distance, like a gazelle.

The school itself reminded Guido of an art gallery, without the beautiful paintings.

Here the walls were stark white, and the tile and furniture nondescript. Your eye could not help but go to the stylists and the hair work in progress.

The styling was the focus, the only focus, the only thing your eye saw.

Gerber looked over Guido, "He's a nice boy, nice looking."

"Now Guido," he said placing his hand on Guido's shoulder, "I have other people here from France and England on a visa. I was able to extend their visa when they joined the beauty school. It's something to think about."

Gerber, Donato, and Guido toured the school for half an hour, leisurely walking the halls to stop and enter classrooms.

The girls, and I say girls, because with few exceptions all were female, and like all females they find Italian men irresistible on some level, although none can explain exactly why.

In one, they were dying hair various shades of red. In another, explaining the intricacies of a layered cut.

"Everyone, this is Guido from Italy, and he's looking at possibly joining us," said Dr. Gerber.

Gerber's eyes looked to Guido so he could speak. Guido said simply, "Cheerio, everyone," in a combination of Italian and English accents.

The girls' eyes darted from Donato, who they knew very well and word had already spread he was on the hunt for a new assistant, and then to Guido, with eyes that said to him, "You're cute, and single."

In the hall, Gerber turned to face Guido, staring him in the eye in a friendly way, "Now I've been showing you the school and talking for most of half an hour, and you haven't said anything!"

"My English is not too good."

"That doesn't matter, everybody helps everybody here. What do you do during the day?"

"I cook the meals at night, and I help care for the kids at my brother Frank's home."

Said Gerber, "Tell you what, why don't you come and spend a day with us at the school. Walk around. Get to know the place. Maybe you'll find it's a good fit. It's a good use of your time, no? Better than staying at home. Hmm?"

And it was that basic common sense approach that attracted Guido, it *was* a better use of time during the day, and as a farm boy Guido knew that time was everything; time to care for the crops, time to harvest, time to eat, time to sleep, always always something to be done to keep the family, the team, going. It was a habit and as much a part of him as his full head of dark hair, or piercing eyes, or nose "like a raven."

That night, Donato told Frank and his wife all about what had happened at the school, about Dr. Gerber and the classes and the Visa, summing up with, "Hey, I think we can get Guido to stay in America if he goes to the school."

Frank knew his brother Guido as well as any human being can know another.

"Look, you want to go to this school? We'll lend you the money you need, the $1200, and you pay us back when you start to work. Ok?"

Later that night, Frank's wife said, "That's a lot of money, Frank."

"You're right, it is. But if he says he wants to go to the school, he'll make it work, and believe me, he'll make it pay, and he'll pay back every penny."

Guido arrived early at the front door of the school two days later wearing a cream colored shirt with gold and black tie, and dark pants with a small notebook and pen in his right hand.

"I decided to take your advice," Guido told Dr. Gerber when the schoolmaster greeted him inside the school.

Guido said little, did what he was asked to do, and listened intently.

As he was leaving Guido in a class, Dr. Gerber asked, "One thing Guido, you have any experience with hair already? I'm just curious."

"Back home, my friends asked me to cut their hair. But it was just a favor, I never charged anything."

Gerber smiled and began walking away, then turned to ask, "Do you think they liked the haircuts?"

"Well, they came back."

Gerber liked Guido's common sense and simplicity. He thought, "This Guido is a practical man."

As Guido walked the halls and sat in on Rita's coloring class, with laughter of young women around him, Guido thought of the endless hours of backbreaking work on the soil with his brothers in Italy; the dirt in his hands and the thirst in the fields, and the pieces of burlap over his shoes to keep the dirt out, and how the land owner took half of the harvest but did no work.

How he promised himself he'd find something better.

"Hair styling is nice and clean and I'd get to work inside, and I get to be with nice ladies."

"The girls, and more important their mothers, enjoy you Guido. They like your sense of humor," his mother had said.

The question was, was styling hair his talent?

"The Satchel"

THE COURTING OF VINCENZA/ PART I
(The Satchel)

The International School was on High Street in Akron, Ohio, a nondescript street in a nondescript town like so many other ageing manufacturing havens in America.

Akron, the former center of tire production and its countless jobs for West Virginians and Kentuckians longing for a piece of the American dream, with dangling arms and a fast gait, sometimes drinking hard and more than ready and willing to work for a day's wages.

With its black soot that stained the snow in winter, and tires crafted by worker's hands belt-by-belt, and occasional vile chemical odors which hung like a cloud of locusts over only the lower-priced neighborhoods laying to the East, as the winds came from the Northwest as a rule.

The school- a hardened, aged red brick structure made from the smaller old style bricks with thin mortar lines made in the day of hand craftsmanship, whose foundation had not budged a quarter inch in over 50 years, kept in good condition by a steady pouring of donations from area immigrants made good who kept the school buzzing with students and a certain energy among both teachers and students reflecting the hopes each student bore deep in his or her heart for something better than home, however cherished, could ever have offered.

And here in this school the languages of far from home and accents and even behavioral eccentricities were twisted like soft rubber into American speech and Americanisms, "everything you need to know to be prepared for life in America," read the brochure.

Guido rode the public bus to school from his brother's home in nearby Barberton, a town created in anger over a match magnate's displeasure with the City of Akron's tax policies.

His one English book had a smashed corner and purplish stain on the side, but this was no problem for a boy who had made do on a farm where improvisation was the daily chant. "I don't complain, it's free!" pretty much summed up his feelings.

So he had his book and his **small leather satchel** his mother had made for him before he left Italy.

He opened the leather packet made of soft reddish leather and touched the items his mother had given him; a stone from the farm, some soil in what had been a miniature perfume bottle of his mother's, a leaf which had already started to crumble, a piece of candy, and her letter.

He opened it and read again what he'd read every day since coming to America.

"My Dearest and Most Beloved Son Guido,

you are not coming back,

I know you think you are coming back, but

the world is bigger for you than for us.

The stone is to remind you how hard it was here

so you don't get homesick,

the dirt to remind you of the smell of your roots,

a leaf to remember there is beauty here,

and a piece of candy to remind you that in the midst

of life's sorrows and sadness there is sweetness,

seek and find the sweetness."

The satchel was his most treasured possession, and it went with him everywhere.

The interior of the school had bland cream tile walls with terrazzo checkered tile floor, hard as any made, polished, with desks and desktops dotted with blue ink stains made of wood seasoned by wear, and rubbing and clasping of hands, and pencils and pens.

There were only 12 in the class, some who could barely speak a word of English, others like himself who had spoken a broken English for years.

Broken words, twisted syllables like irregular pretzels dropped from their mouths, but behind the broken English (most Americans were too quick to criticize or parody) was a soul wise enough and steady enough to find our shores and struggle, usually more successfully than Americans themselves, to find success.

The windows ran across one wall, and next to him in class sat Tony from Bronte in Sicily in the Province of Catania, with endless sun and 78 degree temperatures year-round.

Class was as before, all basic phrases: "Can you direct me to the bathroom? Where is the restaurant?, and, What time is it?"

After class, the two stood by the front of the school waiting for Tony's sister, Vincenza. They were high on the steps, by the metal railing, with a fine view of Tallmadge Avenue surrounded by many hundreds of Italian families and the DeVitis & Sons market down the street with its homemade pasta, little Italian cookies, and green olives in two gallon jars.

"Guido, now listen to me, these crazy Americans, with your English, some will think you're stupid, so what you do is this; when they try to get you to do something you don't want to do, just pretend you don't understand anything they're saying, or maybe even say it back but mix it up a little bit. It works every time!"

And then Guido saw her- she was wearing a grayish-blue dress, mid-calf in length, with a white collar and black shoes. Conservative, but attractive, with an armful of books. Vincenza was 22 but looked more like 18, small of stature and slender.

As she walked up Tony said, "This is Guido, we're in class together."

Vincenza did not look into Guido's face, but gazed just a bit to his right, like the pose from an 18th century painted portrait, in a way which was not rude at all, but reflected a quiet respect for others and absolutely no desire to bring attention to herself.

"She's got a great figure," said Guido to himself, as he stared at her straight dark shoulder length hair curving around a full and smiling face.

As they stood, some of Vincenza's girlfriends walked by, and as they did so, each spoke to her, "Goodbye Vincenza, see you on Wednesday." "You did good in class today Vincenza." It was obvious she was well-liked by the girls, and more than one stared at Guido with eyes that indicated interest. Guido did not look back at them.

Vincenza nodded to each girl passing and Guido wondered if she would speak to him again, and when the crowd of girls might pass.

Then Tony said they had to go and he started walking away. Vincenza hesitated next to Guido, as if she was going to speak to him, but didn't. She just smiled and nodded her head, and quickly joined her brother.

Guido watched them walk away, their figures getting smaller and smaller in the picture of Tallmadge Avenue.

In some way he could not explain, he felt that Vincenza was the same as his mother. Not for certain, just a hint of a feeling, a sense, but it was something he thought about several times in the weeks ahead, so far from home and his family's love.

THE COURTING OF VINCENZA/ PART II

He came to the home of Vincenza often, and she would greet him at the door with a smile.

Under his arm would be homemade bread, or homemade wine, or some pieces of fruit for her and her parents, Alfio and Nunzia Ciraldo.

He would sit with Vincenza's father and brother in the living room, talking of life in Sicily, while Vincenza and her mother would prepare foods in the kitchen.

"He seems like a nice boy," Nunzia said.

"Yes, he is," Vincenza answered.

"I think he's going to ask to marry you."

Vincenza did not speak but from the look in her eyes her mother knew her daughter would say yes.

At dinner, Guido and Vincenza would be seated side-by-side, and he might squeeze her hand, or try to steal a kiss in the home, which was not easy with everyone around.

For Guido, a woman had to meet a very specific set of criteria reflecting guidance from his mother and grandmother, and from the sum of his own life's experience.

She had to be family-oriented, not run around with other guys, and he had to like her.

Vincenza ranked high on all. She was a dutiful daughter, not afraid of work, and had never dated any men or boys.

Her personality was on the quiet side and reserved, but you could tell she had a warmth to her. When she wanted to correct a person, she would not blast away like a cannon, but would search for a calm and considerate way of saying whatever needed to be said, and Guido took this as a sign of *Grace*.

Guido was also concerned about anything that looked flashy, be that clothing or nail color, and did not like girls who wanted to go to expensive restaurants or shopped at expensive stores, wore too much jewelry, or evidenced a selfish attitude.

It was with great surprise a month later that Guido found Vincenza's father no longer wanted him at their house.

"I heard that his family drinks, and so he's not welcome," he said to Nunzia. And with that, Vincenza's father left the house and walked quickly to the corner bar.

When Guido arrived, Vincenza told him her father had left and what he'd said.

Guido sat waiting for hours.

At last, Vincenza's father returned.

Guido looked him in the eye..."If you have a problem with me or my family you should speak to me about it and let me address it."

Vincenza's father just looked at his shoes, too embarrassed to speak, and he knew Guido was right.

Later that night, Vincenza's mother asked her husband, "Why did you do this?"

"Someone said his family drinks."

"They drink wine at dinner like us, that's all. Don't listen to people who don't know what they're talking about."

"Vincenza likes Guido and he's going to ask her to marry him and she's going to say yes, so you'd best treat him well, or that's the end of that," she said with a stern look, indicating the impending loss of gentleman's privileges in the bedroom.

He thought about it and said, "It's no problem, no problem, OK, I'm saying no problem."

"Besides," he said, "I like the fact that Guido stood his ground and waited for me to return, and spoke honestly." Then he added, "He acts like a man, and he will make something of himself."

THE BREAD HEIST

Living with his brother, Frank, and Frank's wife Carmela, was a pleasant life for Guido.

It was a comfortable, small town street in Barberton with row after row of nondescript, vinyl-sided homes, sometimes with a bit of aged, red brick facing, sometimes not.

Next door lived Uncle John and his wife Antonietta, with an alley between the two homes just wide enough so that if you extended your arms out you could just touch both homes with your fingertips.

The kind of town you can raise a family in safely...small town America.

A drive-by in the neighborhood at night would reveal family after family in silhouette in their living rooms illuminated by the bluish flicker of TV screen light, music of various styles, or cries and giggles of kids playing and laughing.

Guido had his own room with a small closet having a single rod upon which hung the 7 pieces of clothing he owned: one suit coat, various pants, and a few shirts.

Each day, he helped with the cooking and spent hours playing with the children, teaching them games or telling them stories of his life on the farm. Their favorites being, *The Electric* Cat, and *The Drunk Cow*.

At night, the two families would gather for a game of cards over prosciutto and homemade wine, talking Italian except for the occasional colloquialism in English.

On this particular evening Guido had visited Vincenza's family and upon leaving had been given a freshly-baked loaf of bread to take home to Frank's wife, which he held carefully on his lap on the bus.

His hands turned in and rolled the end of the bag, over and over, until it was firm and gave a good grip.

Off the bus at 11:00 pm and Guido started the ½ mile walk to his brother, Frank's home. The bag of bread swung from his hand and arm like a workman's lunchbox as he took generous strides towards the house on 15th Street. He walked across the crosswalk, and was ready to cross the street to Frank's home.

The night air held crisp fragrant smells of fresh cut grass, and a few little bits of grass were sticking to his shoe tops.

Tap tap of his shoes on the sidewalk...almost home.

The five toughs sat in their car on the side street, waiting for rubber factory workers coming home on Friday nights with their cash in their pockets from paychecks. Their black car, dull and unattended in appearance, with months of trash on the floor, areas damp from slopped pop and the window left open in a rainstorm days ago, and a slumped suspension caused by a bad spring.

Packed like mongrel puppies in a stinking tipping crate, two up front and three glaring at each other in the back seat.

"This car ain't big enough for three in back," said one.

"Shut up."

"Same as before?," said the young one with straight oily hair in his eyes, up front.

"Yeah," said the blonde-haired leader with pinkish skin and freckles at the wheel of the car, a cigarette dangling absent-mindedly in his right hand with the bandaged thumb.

"We pick one, a little chicken, then YOU go up and grab what they got. Then, I pull up and you hop in. Comin' from the rubber shops with their little pay and we're gonna share it with 'em. If they give us any trouble, we'll all jump out and pound 'em good."

"I think we should split it 5 ways this time," came a voice from the backseat, munching on a candy bar.

"Naw, I take half like last time, you guys split the rest."

"That ain't fair."

"To hell with your fair, I'm the leader and someday when you got your own gang then you take half, just like me."

And so the slumped black car with its two big round headlights sat waiting for a "chicken," while the one in back chewed his candy.

Guido stopped to cross the street and saw the black car approaching, saw it pass him and stop at the stop sign, and saw Nance step out.

Guido kept on walking 20 steps from the house.

Nance quickly walked towards Guido, shoved him hard and grabbed the brown paper bag, pulling it from Guido's arms.

As Nance began to run to the car, now down the street to the left of the crosswalk, Guido caught him by the shirt and pulled hard- hard enough to tear the shirt off.

Nance lost his footing, fell back and hit his head hard on a fire hydrant, and Guido could hear the thump of this head as Nance yelled, "Help!"

The mongrel toughs hopped out of their car and chased Guido through the narrow alley to Frank's backyard with its vegetable gardens.

"No time to get the key in the door and get in the house," thought Guido as he raced to the tomato plant stakes, and began pulling them up for a weapon. But they were all tied up with string and would not come apart.

The four threw Guido to the ground and began beating him and kicking him. Guido could smell the fresh cut grass as he made himself into a ball on the ground.

"Frank, get a gun and shoot these sons of bitches," Guido yelled, and then yelled again louder.

Lights went on in the house, and a dog two doors down erupted in howls.

The toughs ran like wild mustangs through the backyard, into the car. The car lurched back to get Nance, still lying by the hydrant, with the bread next to him in its bag.

"Get in! Get in," they yelled as he groggily made his way to the car.

They grabbed Nance by his belt and with the door still open, started pulling away.

Guido was on Nance, and grabbed him also by the belt, his feet sliding on the pavement.

A tug of war for Nance ensued down the street as the car careened, first to one side-then the other, hoping to drop Guido and free Nance.

Finally, Guido could hold no longer. Nance was in, the door slammed shut, and the black car with mongrels intact sped away down the street, lights off.

Guido was wet with sweat and could not make out the license plate in the dark as the engine's howl faded into the night.

"What the hell are you doing?," screamed Frank as he ran up.

"They tried to steal my bread."

"Your bread? What are you nuts? They could have had a gun."

Guido walked slowly back to the hydrant and picked up the loaf of bread, still in pristine condition. He smoothed the paper and went inside to give it to Carmela.

She said, "Go look in the mirror."

He looked and saw green streaks and dirt on his pants and shirt from the tussle.

"Yeah, I see, but they didn't get the bread."

THE CONTEST

Jessica had a beautifully-shaped oval face, dark brown hair with just a hint of curl, and kind brown eyes to augment her happy, go-lucky personality. Perfect for the model Guido would need to enter the Gerber Beauty School's annual competition for seniors. He hoped to win one of the three top place ribbons.

The problem was, Guido was a freshman, and had only been in the school for a few months. But Rita Maco, head colorist teacher at the school, who liked Guido, arranged for him to enter, explaining to the head of the school, "I honestly don't think he knows it's for seniors only, and his English is so poor that I'm not sure I can explain it to him, and I don't want to hurt his feelings. It's really easier to let him in the competition, he won't win anyway, so no harm will be done."

Rita's husband, Joe was very familiar with his wife's ways. He thought to himself that either she liked Guido, or had been swayed by his small farm background in Italy, or was looking to put the sting to Donna, the bright red-haired hairstylist who had already proclaimed *she* herself would win first place. Donna, the same monster he'd heard about for a week who had the audacity to take the school's curlers home without permission, and had walked away from Rita's admonitions muttering, "Hey, it's no big deal. Chill out."

Rita had always noted Guido's dutiful attitude, lack of talking back, and ease in all things.

Rita had seen that Guido could "do" anything immediately upon being shown. His gentle hands working quickly and efficiently, curling, cutting, to the point where Rita was actually having him demonstrate technique to the other students.

But the girls were not jealous. Each held a desire to hug and squeeze Guido, like a puppy dog, and his Italian background was considered one more plus in his column.

Nancy Ferguson's comment, the student considered most beautiful, summed up how most of the girls felt, and solidified Guido's position firmly as favorite: "I don't care if he can't talk English...most of what boys say bores me anyway, and he's cute."

On the day of the contest, all the 30 competing students were at their chairs spaced on the outside walls on the periphery of the main hair working area, with their model in a chair in front of them, and a large arch-shaped mirror in front of the chair, each mirror surrounded with broken black and tan tiles creating an outer decorative arch.

"You look so pretty I'm just gonna pretend to cut your hair, and you still win," Guido said to Jessica. It calmed her and she smiled warmly ready to begin.

"Go," said Rita, as all began with a shampoo and rinse, to relax the hair and allow it to fall so that the maximum styling methods could be applied.

Rita walked the room, and as she did so Donna the redhead said loudly enough to be heard, "I don't think Guido is a senior, is he a senior? He shouldn't be competing at all."

Rita picked up her speed and walked right on by, turning her head to survey the other students.

Guido had chosen to create a look which, while stylish and current (hair a bit shorter on one side than the other), was still well within the confines of good and appropriate taste.

("When you cut a woman's hair, don't make it for your ego, give them something they will feel good about," his cousin Donato had told him many times.)

It was a blind contest, meaning each chair had a number and the judge, Lola Vincent, the grande dame of the largest hair cutting syndicate in the U.S., S&L, was Chief Judge.

To the surprise of many, after the shampooing and clipping and cutting and air blowing and fussing, Guido won third place, and the girls all clapped when they heard.

"A nice group, hmmm?," said Rita to Lola, "Anyone of interest?," which was her shorthand for who would be offered a job with S&L.

"I want to talk to the Italian boy who won third," Lola said in a very cool tone, which Rita knew meant any discussion of jobs for other students was out until Lola finished with Guido. Rita had three from the school she wanted hired, and they'd get jobs, she was sure, but she'd wait.

Rita took Guido by the arm to Lola, and then stood some 9 feet away, pretending to be looking at a favorite student's work, touching the model's hair, saying to the stylist Amy, "Next year you'll probably win."

"So, tell me about yourself," Lola said, and Guido noticed that as he spoke the cool businesswoman's veneer melted like the early snows in Fossalto, and he saw a smiling warm face that reminded him of his mother's best friend, Teresa, who lived two farms down from their own farm in Italy."

"I'm from Italy, my family is from Fossalto. I have 8 brothers and sisters, I'm living with my brother, Frank's family in Barberton and my mother and father and my grandmother and some of my brothers and sisters are still in Italy, on the farm.

(Silence) What else?," he said with a warm smile.

"You have a job offer yet?" she asked as she twirled her pen in her perfectly manicured fingers.

"I have only been in the school for a few months. I'm here on a Visa, and then I'm to return to England, and then perhaps back home to Italy."

She watched his eyes intently as she spoke, "Well, when you want a job I want you to call me, and I will get you a job...a job in England, or Italy, or here in America."

"Now if you work for us in Europe and want to come back to America to visit for several months or longer, I can arrange that by getting you an instructor's visa," she said as she handed him her business card.

Lola had made her decision regarding Guido quickly, and she had acted in the manner her reputation said she would; with strength and finality. After all, she was Lola Vincent.

And what she said next was certainly not business advice and was not taken as such by Guido. She took his hand, and held and squeezed it, saying, "You know what I'd do....I'd find a nice American girl." Then she turned and walked away.

From that moment on at the school, things changed for Guido. He was no longer the young boy from Italy who spoke halting English, or the one who needed help.

He was an *extremely gifted* student who had a wonderful career in front of him with S&L, and they were *lucky* to have him...someone who could help their own careers move forward.

After a short private talk with Rita in the office, Donna the redhead fawned over Guido, and did all she could to help him humanly possible, to the point that everyone would have thought she had a crush on him, but for the strongly held belief that Donna seemed disposed towards females.

MARY COLLINS...MY FIRST CLIENT

Lola Vincent hired Guido the moment he called her, remembering him from the contest, and was very pleased he'd chosen to stay in the United States.

"We're lucky to have you," she'd said.

He started at the downtown Polsky's location in Akron, Ohio, on Main Street.

It was the busiest street in town...a collection of mismatched buildings built over a century, evidencing many architectural styles.

The store, a highly-regarded shopping destination, was known for their men's and women's clothing, their Christmas displays locals came to see like a shrine of sorts, and the hairstylists on the lower floor.

It was Guido's first day. He had no customers or appointments, and he'd been sitting in the lounge some time, reading, as being new he had to wait for an "up"- someone who came in the door with no appointment.

Janet Singles was hungry, and as a senior stylist, when she wanted to eat she just left.

"You have Mary Collins at 10:00," Elsie, the peepmouse girl at the front desk warned.

"I don't care and I'm hungry, she's always late anyway, and she complains all time. I'm sick of her," said Janet as she slammed the glass door on the rubber floor stop.

At 10:00 sharp Mary arrived wondering once again how she was going to try to explain to this numbskull hairstylist exactly what she wanted done with her hair.

She didn't like Janet's work at all, but the truth was, she'd been through so many hairstylists, she just didn't have the heart to begin hunting anew.

"What do you mean Janet isn't here? I have an appointment at 10:00," said Mary.

Elsie just looked at the book, peering down.

"Just pick someone else, I don't care who," Mary intoned.

Elsie went in back and asked Guido if he wanted Mary.

Guido walked in, said hello to Mary Collins and asked Elsie, "Can I fit her into my schedule?"

"You have 45 minutes until your next appointment," Elsie said.

"Come right this way," he said as he walked her to his station.

He placed the hair cape around her, and felt a bit self-conscious, a bit nervous.

She was his *first* customer.

He could tell by her bearing that she was a woman of importance in town, and her clothing was expensive but conservative.

Odd, she was not rude to Guido in the least. She listened attentively to the stories of his life on the farm, and his life in England, laughing and telling him about her upbringing.

Her father had built a success from nothing, and she and her husband had risen to local prominence by good old-fashioned hard work, and an Ohioan's no-nonsense work ethic.

She explained what she had in mind for her hair, and Guido tried to give it to her to the best of his ability.

When he was done he handed her the mirror and Mary looked carefully.

She looked on one side, then swiveled the chair to the other side, then back again to the other side, and this went on and on for several minutes.

After a silence, she said, "This is the first time in my life someone cut my hair exactly the way I want it. I'm going to send you business."

And she did. In fact her referrals created enough work to secure him as one of the busiest stylists in the shop in very little time as Mary made it a point to go to all the women who'd ever complained about their stylist, saying, "I'm telling you, Doris, you will not believe what he will do. He's a genius."

In 6 months he was fully booked every day.

Getting her things together after her first cut, Mary went to pay at the desk. She asked Guido, "Can you fit me in every week?"

He said to Elsie, "See what you can do."

Mary Collins was a customer for 40 years.

THE ENGAGEMENT

Guido looked at his image in the mirror for some time, turning this way and that, adjusting his tie, taming his hair and eyebrows, before heading to dinner at Vincenza's home, for tonight was the night he would ask her to marry him.

He dusted the lint from his brown checkered sport coat made by a tailor from his hometown in Fossalto, inspected his black pants and freshly-polished black shoes, felt for the ring in its box in his pocket for the seventh time, and picked up the flowers.

It was one of the biggest days in his life, and his *sole regret* was that his mother and father were not here to see it and enjoy it too.

Vincenza was everything he wanted in a wife- beautiful, caring, tactful, responsible, and respectful. He'd known these things from the day he first met her outside the school where English was taught.

He knew she would say yes, could tell from the look in her dark eyes when he looked at her, holding her hand.

It was Thanksgiving day, and Vincenza met him at her father's house in a burgundy colored dress, with a burgundy and white collar.

Vincenza could tell from his expression at the door that something was up.

They'd been dating for six months, and had seen each other every other day for that entire time.

Stolen kisses in the kitchen, at the door, and both felt it was time that they no longer had to steal kisses.

Around the table, Vincenza's entire family was seated: 3 brothers, her mother and father, and Guido's brother Frank and his wife, Carmela, and Uncle John and his wife Antonietta.

Guido rose to speak.

"Hello everybody. Vincenza and I have talked for quite a while now. We are in love, and we want to get married. I'm lucky to find a good family in you, a family like mine. So, I'm going to propose, but one thing...I want to ask the permission of the parents...I would like permission to marry your daughter."

They nodded, not really speaking, but the smiles around the table indicated he was welcome to the family.

"So," Guido said, lifting her by her hand from the chair, "Would you like to marry me?"

She said yes, and they kissed on the lips in front of everyone. Then he put the ring on her finger.

Vincenza played with the ring all through dinner, turning it around her finger, touching it, and looking at it, even as she lay in bed that night trying to go to sleep.

Guido and Vincenza were married on January 2nd, 1965, in St. Anthony's Church in Akron. 300 guests attended.

He lifted the wedding cake to her lips respectfully, and acted the gentleman in all ways possible.

LIFE LESSONS

CHALLENGES IN MARRIAGE... COMMUNICATION

Communication.

I think there are things even a wife and husband do not want to say to each other...yet if you don't say them, you'll start resenting it.

Then one partner holds a grudge, and it leads to other things.

Something small can make you snap, like not washing a dish. The problem wasn't the dish, your partner is upset about something else-perhaps something you should have talked about from the past, but did not.

I've been married 48 years, and even now, there are things I don't want to say.

Communication is very important, but I didn't say it was easy!

A FOCUS ON HOME

"When I was pregnant with our first child, Emilio, I quit my job doing draperies," said Vincenza, so she could focus 100% of her life and time with the children.

She was there to care for them, to feed them, and see them grow each day. They held onto her legs while she cooked, and stood on their tip toes on her feet, until she'd say, "Now, off, off," with a pat on their heads.

Guido had moved his business to an area attached to their home and thus was able to be there for the children each day. The children could run in and see their father, ask questions and help with things like sweeping the floor. They learned to contribute to the family early on, and never lacked for their father's voice or counsel.

Yet many people questioned why Vincenza did not continue to work, in the heyday of woman's liberation.

"How can you make your wife care for the children all day?," they'd ask Guido, "She has a life too, and a career."

"As I see it," said Guido, "I have to work all day, and so it's natural that my wife take care of the children, and she is a wonderful mother. If the children wake at night, she cares for them, yet she can take a nap with the children when they are napping during the day, and catch up on her sleep."

"It makes no sense to hire a baby sitter for my wife to work because the babysitter is earning $10 an hour, and to hold a job you have to buy clothes and gas and a car."

"I think in American society (and this is very different from Italy), many people, successful people, don't want to be home all day raising the kids."

"Some come to find there is a price to pay for not being home as much," said Guido.

BOULDERS AROUND THE LAKE
(As related by Emilio Cornacchione, eldest son of Guido and Vincenza)

We have a small lake in our backyard, and my papa decided that to stop the pussy willows from growing all around it each year (creating a mucky bottom), that he'd put rocks around it.

My brother Carlo and I came home from school one day to see a huge mound of broken concrete in the parking lot a good distance from the lake.

Papa had us put plastic down around the entire edge of the lake, extending into the water and up the bank, and then said we were to pick up the rocks and transport them to the water's edge, and put them on the plastic...all the way around.

Carlo and I looked at each other and said we couldn't pick up the rocks and carry them, as they were huge chucks of concrete, and too heavy. "Use the wheelbarrow," Papa answered.

After a couple of weeks, we asked, "Why didn't you put the rocks closer to the lake? Why do we have to carry them so far?"

"That's where the rocks were dropped off by the man who brought them here," he said.

Every day, we'd work to carry those chunks of concrete and they were heavy, with the wheelbarrow occasionally tipping over.

Our friends were having fun after school, playing, but we worked "the quarry."

One day, we'd had enough. We went into Papa's shoppe and said, "We quit, we're not doing this anymore...it's too hot, it's too hard. Our friends don't have to do it at their homes."

Papa looked at us and didn't speak or respond at all for some time.

Then he said, "You're not looking at it right. Now you see the difficulty and the sweat, but in years ahead- and there will be many years ahead- you'll look with pride at your work, and feel good each time you look at the clean water's edge all around, and you'll enjoy the water."

My brother and I had no response, just looked at each other and went back to work.

"Look at that edge," Emilio said as he showed me his work with a sweep of his arm, now a man of 38.

"My brother and I put every rock in place...and I'm really proud of it...look at it."

"I didn't really understand what my papa was saying until I was an adult. When young, I was the one getting into trouble doing this and that. But now, I see clearly what Papa was saying."

Emilio married his wife Donina in 2010, and they now have two children, Aria and Enzo.

ADIOS

He came to my shoppe, and talked while I cut his hair.

"I'm having problems with my wife," he said of the woman, 23 years younger.

"I can't figure out why my marriage is not working," he said perplexed.

He was successful and in a prestigious position in the community.

I told him, "You are choosing girls which are too young because of their looks and their young age."

In my view they weren't with him because they loved him, but for his prestige and money.

And he was letting them make a lot of expensive decisions.

He was compensating, and now she wanted him to pay for an expensive vacation overseas.

"She's my third wife, I don't want to split up, I don't want to lose this marriage," he said.

"Let's look back," I said. "She wanted a big wedding, but you said you wanted just a few relatives. She insisted, but you didn't ask her if she had any money to put towards this wedding she wanted."

"She doesn't have any money," he said.

"I would have said, 'if you have no money to contribute, there will be no big wedding.' If she says adios just because you won't pay for an expensive wedding, you're lucky."

She left him a year later.

It was adios.

ON DATING AND SEX WHEN YOUNG

If a young girl wants to go out with someone, they need to go out as a group, 4, or 5, or 6 of them together.

A young woman needs to be 17 or 18 to go on a date one-on-one.

Sex at 11 or 12 years of age?

I think it's wrong. I don't know why it's happening.

Go to a fast food restaurant, and while you eat, people are having sex on TV.

The worst part is that young people really don't know what they are doing. They do it because someone else did, or because they want to be accepted.

As I look at families today, half are responsible, and half are not.

When a parent asks me to put highlights in an 11-year-old girl's hair, what does that tell you?

She is not old enough for fashion, but parents pay the money.

Kids get cars they couldn't afford on their own, and are given insurance, and even money.

And a lot of that gets misused, on drugs and on alcohol.

Too many parents treat the kids like they are their friends.

Like they want the children to like them.

That's 100% wrong. Kids and adults want discipline, they want to be told.

If you confront them with their incorrect behaviors, and you are right and make some sense, you get more respect by speaking up and fulfilling your parental role than by not saying anything.

EMILIO'S FLAT TIRE
(As related by Emilio Cornacchione)

My car had a flat tire, and I left it at the mall...about a mile and a half from home.

That night, I went out partying with friends.

The next morning, I slept till 11:00, then went to talk with Papa in his shoppe.

"Papa, I need a ride to work."

"No," he said, "You went out last night, and chose to not fix the flat. I was working when you came home last night, and I'm working now, so you walk to work."

It was a long walk, and that was the last time I didn't fix a flat.

HOME AS A CENTER FOR FAMILY & ACTIVITIES

Something I enjoy, and my family enjoys, is that we've set up a large backyard recreation area with a lake and two outdoor bocci courts, a small kitchen with grille just inside the house, and a gazebo (and one indoor bocci court).

Our home is a center for recreation and enjoying family and friends.

We enjoy looking at it, caring for the landscaping, and preparing food.

It's common in Europe and Canada, and it's a peaceful and relaxing thing.

People walk and jog around the lake, and I get my exercise by working in the garden, which has the advantage over an exercise facility in that you've accomplished something.

Many Italians and Europeans live this way because they are family-oriented.

A house is not an artistic pristine thing. For us, it's a place for people to enjoy friends and family.

Yes, our home gets a bit dirty, with all the people coming and going, but it cleans up quickly. And I used a lot of hard tiles as flooring for fast cleanup...which also keeps the house cooler in summer.

Why do people want a showcase home if they're not going to live and entertain in it?

I honestly don't know.

BOCCI...LEARN FROM THE WAY OTHERS PLAY

We were so busy working on the farm in Italy, that I played bocci only at festivities.

But here in America, I enjoy a game of bocci as often as once a day.

There is a 12 foot by 60 foot court, bordered on all sides by boards 6 to 8 inches high, off which the balls can bounce, and each team has 4 balls. To score, you place your team's balls as close to the little white ball, the pallino, as you can, and move their balls away from the pallino...when you can.

I've learned you can tell more about people's personalities by playing a game of bocci or cards, than from most other activities, because you can learn from what they do, not just what they say.

It helps me figure out what they are made of in a relaxed and friendly way.

If they are fair, or, if they cheat, it tells you something about their personality.

Again, in the game of bocci, actual points are scored by placing the larger balls next to the point ball, or pallino.

If it's close, you measure. Many times one player will strongly state their ball is closer. They may repeat themselves, then pout or grump in other ways if it's not called their way.

"You don't mind if I measure?," I ask with a smile.

Many times players are wrong.

Perhaps their eyesight is off.

LET THEM WIN TOO

Naturally, we all want to win at games. But when you don't win, be gracious.

When you win, you want others to be gracious to you. The same is true for them.

I feel good if you congratulate me when I win, and so I congratulate people when they win.

Keep games fun and friendly, but with a sense of humor. Joke around and don't get offended.

Some seem mad at the world.

Games are entertainment, it's supposed to be fun.

I almost don't like to beat the ones who are poor losers.

Sometimes I get beaten, and sometimes I let them win, so they can smile.

INAPPROPRIATE BEHAVIOR...
NIP IT IN THE BUD

A friend of Emilio's came over to our home to pick him up.

"He's upstairs changing, he'll be down in a moment," said my wife.

"Oh, I'll go up," he said, while my wife said again, "He will be down in a moment."

He ignored her and started going towards the stairs.

"Where are you going?," I asked him. "Step back."

"Since when is this your house? My wife told you two times he'll be down. Now, you wait until he comes down," I told him.

This tells me what kind of a friend he was for my son. What kind of an attitude he had, and what he was taught at his home.

I suggested that my son spend less time with this boy, who it turned out was 5 years older than my son.

Another time we had a large holiday party, and a friend of my daughter, Rita, was leaning on the doorway into the house, smoking.

I'd posted signs which said "No Smoking."

When I passed him again, he was still smoking in the doorway.

"Excuse me, I don't know if you saw the sign. You cannot smoke here."

When I again passed him, he was still smoking in the same spot.

"You probably didn't hear what I said, there's no smoking."

"Yeah, I heard you," he said.

He didn't like being told what to do.

"You heard me and didn't do what I asked, and didn't do a thing about it, which is worse yet. This is my place and you are moving from this spot, now."

It's been my experience that allowing inappropriate behavior, without correction, just results in more inappropriate behavior, until the problem escalates to where you *must* take action.

A swift and respectful correction works wonders, and I've found that those I correct respect me afterwards.

PRICE OF WINES

To my mind, the difference between wines isn't huge, but the pricing can be.

When you get right down to it, wine has grape juice, sugar, and alcohol, which only cost so much.

If you like the taste, there is nothing wrong with a less expensive sweet wine.

I think people get too focused on a name brand. Sometimes the reason price is higher is that they make less quantity-it's supply and demand.

A $200 bottle doesn't taste any better than an average wine to me.

When I can buy a *gallon* of blended wine for $12, and the *bottle* of single harvest vintage is $8, I don't mind the mix. We mixed wines often in Italy to improve the flavor.

In this economy, when you start thinking about how you spend your money, you may start thinking differently.

LISA'S SWISS CHEESE CAR

Lisa, with her beautiful dark hair and slender figure, was going to high school and working at a country club to save her money for college.

I bought her a good car, it was $300 and was a yellow Chevy Vega. It ran well but had a lot of holes. As you'll remember, they were prone to rust.

She drove the car to school the first day, came home, and I heard her slam the car door.

I asked her, "What is it?"

"Nothing."

"What's the problem?," I asked her.

"I'm not driving this car anymore."

"Why," I asked, "Is there something wrong with the car?"

"The kids made fun of it. They called it Swiss Cheese."

"Now let's talk about this," I said.

"You don't want to drive the car because people say it's swiss cheese?"

She nodded.

"I believe if I had the money, I still wouldn't buy a new car, but we don't have the money."

"On the bright side, you don't have to walk to work, you can drive. And if it is swiss cheese it's pretty good looking swiss cheese.

And, I think the guys are not looking at the car, they're looking at the really good looking girl in the car."

She decided to drive the car.

Two to three days later, the swiss cheese car had made the popularity list. Everyone wanted to ride in "the swiss cheese car."

The moral of the story is...outcome depends how you approach things.

GETTING TOGETHER WITH OTHERS

I put a lot of time and energy into putting together groupings of people I and my family like to be with.

With today's busy schedules, this is not easy. Somebody has to be in charge, most of the time that's me.

In 1989, we started to spend time with friends, and it was a hit or miss thing.

People didn't seem able to make it.

Then, I changed the approach.

We chose couples and picked one night of the week for all of us to get together for cards.

With a definite date each week, people began showing up on a consistent basis.

It's amazing to me, it's been 17 years, and we all cancelled only twice.

And we are so close, the group is like family.

If we play a card game, when we lose, we put the money in a pot, and at the end of the season the dollars pay for a party where we bring all our families together.

MUSINGS ABOUT ITALY

Italy is a very pretty country in the sense of picturesque mountains, hills, and little villages up on a hill. So to look at it, even from far away, it's very picturesque.

Much of Italy has seasons similar to Ohio. Northern Italy is cold in winter with snow, where Sicily is like Florida...warm and sunny.

Italy is a destination point for tourists.

It has so many things. People come to see the Vatican and its 16 chapels, and when it comes to antiquity, there is so much old architecture to enjoy in what is an ancient country.

Venice is a city built on water and the water comes right around the buildings.

People don't have a street. When they go out, they take a boat- right out their front door.

Once six of us took a train and drove to Venice. Once you get in the area of the city, you can't drive. You park and walk.

Your taxi is a boat.

Italy is a nice country. People are warm, and they tend to be a happier people.

People sing out their windows, and when we walked along, we sang.

There is more violence now.

Italians used to go to live all around the world, to Switzerland and Belgium, but not so much anymore.

Italy is known for its fashion. People like to wear the latest styles in clothing and hairstyles.

90% of the people get a new suit each year, and it's in the most current style.

Italians are affectionate, and family is still close knit. More so than in America.

Italy is well-known for food. It's said Americans eat to live, but Italians live to eat.

We eat with purpose, because we think eating is a good thing to do, and a family activity.

I've been to so many American homes where they offer you no food and no drink.

In an Italian family, when you go visit, they don't even ask. Out comes the vino, the salami, and treats.

The first time I went to England, I had a date with a girl and I took a bus to the house.

I rang the bell, and her mother came and opened the door. "She'll be right down, the rest of the family is eating dinner," she said.

Then she suggested I sit with them while they ate, and they never offered me anything. No food, no beverage, nothing.

"You got to be kidding me," I thought.

In Italy we eat a lot of fruits, and wine.

In America, we eat a lot of steaks.

In Italy, we mostly eat the younger beef, or veal.

Italy and America, they are different and I hope you go visit Italy to see.

TEN BURNER STOVE FOR A SONG

When you raise a large family on a limited income (just like living on a farm), you learn to get the most from every dollar.

We needed a ten burner gas stove for a second kitchen in our home. I wanted it to be a commercial grade addition with large capacity hood and stainless steel counters.

The ad was under home furnishings, "10 burner stove, used to be in our church, now stored in barn."

I bought it along with a pizza oven for $150. The gas stove and pizza oven would have cost about $6,500 new. They took some cleaning up and polishing to look good.

Now we can cook pasta fajoule, potatoes, beans, broken spaghetti, pastina, 3-4 pans of lasagna, and fresh made pizza- all at the same time.

Many people buy new and pay full price.

But you have other options, and in today's economy those options might make the difference between have and have not.

THE APPLE SEEDS AND
GETTING SMARTER

A man by the side of the road has a truck with a sign posted, "Smart Seeds."

By the ground are pieces of apples, with the man cutting seeds from an apple.

"4 seeds, four dollars," the vendor says.

A policeman goes by, and says it's stupid, but goes back and buys the seeds.

He went back to his patrol car, ate the seeds and thought...that was dumb of me to spend $4 for seeds. I could have bought a bushel of apples and had the seeds too.

Back he went to the vendor, as he shared his observations.

"See, you're getting smarter already," said the man selling seeds.

DOING SOMETHING NICE FOR SOMEONE

I had a lady come in today who always had a garden.

"Oh, I didn't plant this year because I have high blood pressure," she said.

I told her I'd go get her some fresh food from my garden, and put some vegetables in her car.

She started to cry, she was so happy.

It was only worth $10, but it was a gesture, and they got something fresh from the garden from their hairstylist.

Often we underestimate the value of a kind word or kindness to another.

RITA AND HER DIRTY UNIFORM
(As related by Rita Cornacchione Brienza)

I got home very late that night from baseball, and was too tired to wash my uniform.

The coach's rules were you couldn't play if your uniform wasn't clean.

I knew it was my responsibility to wash my own uniform, but that night, I just left it out for Mamma.

Mamma didn't see it in the morning.

"Oh my," said Mamma in the morning, "I didn't see your uniform. I'll clean it and take it to school for you."

My papa said, "No, she chose to manipulate you, so she can either not play or she can stay home and wash her own uniform, but she has to figure it out and solve it on her own."

I just took the uniform to school and tried to clean it there, but couldn't get it clean enough.

The coach said my uniform was not clean enough to play. For me that was torture. It was embarrassing.

My uniform was always clean after that, and I cleaned it myself.

HELPING PEOPLE OPEN UP

Whatever I'm saying, I try not to look smarter than other people.

You get more information indirectly, and you'll notice people resent being questioned, especially if you don't know them that well.

First, get a feel for the person and their personality.

I always listen to other people. If for example we are playing a game of cards or bocci, they talk when they get comfortable, and then I learn more about them.

Make people feel welcome, and when they feel relaxed and comfortable, they will feel at home and open up.

DRESS RIGHT

When you go to a family event, dress like the others there. Not too casual.

Be respectful of where you are. It shows respect for others, and minimizes problems.

If you're not sure what the dress code is, then ask someone to guide you.

I find if I'm casual, but nice, I can't go wrong. And, it's always better to be a bit overdressed than underdressed.

Too many times people get so stressed out about how to dress.

All it takes is one question to ask.

Try to know for sure.

EVERYBODY CAN TEACH YOU SOMETHING

I purchased a used leaf blower, the kind you carry on your back.

It would idle, but as soon as you tried to really run it, it would shut off.

I took it to the dealer, "Oh, we can't service this. They don't make it anymore."

While driving, I passed a dumpy little garage by a gas station. There sat a young scruffy man some might call a hillbilly.

He knew the unit.

"It's just a small screen to keep the gas clean. I can fix it."

He took it out, and it was fixed in a minute and a half.

"How much?," I asked.

"Nothing."

I left him $5.

Everybody can teach you something, if you let them.

A DEAL ON A HOUSE

When Giovanni and my daughter, Rita, got married, they began looking for a house.

They told me they'd found a nice brick ranch, but it was a little bit old-fashioned, with older wallpaper and décor.

I thought it was a great place.

I kept telling them, "Don't be scared by the wallpaper, look at the structure of the home."

Another problem was that it only had one bathroom, and I explained that they could offer much less than the asked-for price, and pay to put in a nice bathroom.

In fact, it had been sitting for 6 months with no offer.

In this case, they didn't buy the home, and a man bought it for his mother, and she only needed one bathroom.

If I'd have purchased the home, I'd have added a bathroom and sold it for $20,000 more than I paid for it.

BUY A USED CAR

So far in my life, I haven't bought a new vehicle yet.

The reason is that I believe that as soon as you drive the new car off the showroom floor, or the lot, you lose several thousand dollars-dollars which *you* paid.

I always look for a used RELIABLE car, with about 20-30 thousand miles, and about 2 to 3 years old.

I get a good vehicle for half the price.

I think sometimes people are too concerned about the possibility of repair costs with used cars.

It's true that in some cases you might get a lemon, but these are rare, and a two-year-old car has many of the bugs already worked out.

Even if you do have to pay for some repairs, you will be well-ahead of the money you'll put in to buy new, or lease.

I pay on average about $6,000 for cars.

Large vehicles which get a low number of miles per gallon, like SUVs, are not a problem if you don't drive much, and they make seeing easier.

Plus, they are often four wheel drive, which is a big plus in snowy winter weather.

ON DONATIONS

I have mixed feelings on making donations.

When I do donate, often it's to causes having definite, proven merit, with monies collected by someone I know.

I very seldom make contributions to large organizations, unless I really know that organization well.

One reason is that there are so many hands touching the money.

You'll find many get taken by giving to charities they don't know very well, and that's happening a lot more on the web.

People put together a solicitation to help someone, and we learn the entire story was made up.

Know who you are donating to, and the better you know them- the wiser the move to help.

WATCH OUT WITH CREDIT CARDS

I have a lot of concerns with how credit card companies market their products and services.

The small print is so extensive, it's hard to know what you are committing to.

And there are so many loopholes that if you don't pay attention, you get taken advantage of.

Examples of pitches I find offensive are, "Enjoy that vacation you so badly deserve," with some low introductory interest rate, or "no interest."

The interest bumps up after so many months, and those interest rates are often usurious.

Or, they send you "free checks" and suggest you write one to yourself, but fail to mention there is a 3% fee to write the check buried in the small print.

Some people rotate their balances, to take advantage of lower rates, but if you forget to transfer the debt in time- you can be facing 12% interest rates, or higher.

If you don't pay on time, the rate jumps again.

If you use cards, pay the balance on time in full.

Credit cards are a privilege, and they do have their benefits. But use them wisely.

PURCHASING FOOD

Our experience has been that many times, you can save a considerable amount on food purchases with practices which are risk-free.

As an example, this morning's bread might cost $2, but tomorrow that same loaf will sell for $1.

It's only one day old, and the bread did not spoil.

With produce, such as lettuce, most people pay a premium price. It's worth the time to find lower prices.

With meat, a lower-priced cut of meat is definitely cheaper, but if cooked correctly, it's better for you and has less fat.

A shoulder steak can taste great if you cook it correctly.

It's a strange thing, but people somehow conclude that if it costs less, it won't taste as good.

It's just in your mind.

AMERICA AND ITALY

Once I went back to Italy and to a bank in Rome.

They formed a line, and I was a few places from the teller.

All of a sudden, a man comes in wearing an expensive 3-piece suit and cuts ahead of us in line, handing his transaction to the teller.

I grabbed him by the arm and put him at the back of the line, "You are going to wait here just like we all did."

The teller had taken no action, because in Italy if you are big shot, many times you do what you want.

In Italy, if you want a business telephone, you could wait for 6 months.

And speeding things up is a matter of, "who you know."

And there are a lot of bribes.

Equality under the law. That's one thing I love about America.

NO MEANS NO

One of my grandchildren was staying at our home. He went into the kitchen and opened a cupboard door to take things out.

There was a little pile on the floor.

"Oh, don't say anything," the others said, "let her mother teach her how she wants".

I took his hand and gave it a little spank, "When you are over here, you don't go into the cupboards," I told him.

He never did it again at our home.

MUSIC IN ITALY

Very few people had a chance to take lessons on musical instruments when I was a child. People learned to play an instrument, such as an accordion, on their own, and made things up.

Two of my cousins became very good, and played dance music: polka, waltz, and tango.

They would play and we would sing along, and they were invited to go to homes and play, not as a business, but for the joy of music.

People would sing while they did laundry, or walking around the streets at night.

People didn't have much in those days, but they lived a happier life than today.

Modern conveniences cost money to purchase, such as a car, and they cost money to repair. Paying for all of it can be stressful.

Sometimes, less is more.

BE ON TIME

If you can't be there on time, let the person you are meeting with know. If need be, reschedule.

I have this problem with workmen all the time.

They say a job will be done on a given day, and never show up.

In my opinion, most people would do much better in business if they just followed this one simple rule: be on time.

Physicians seem to suffer from this malady more than most, and I often hear of patients asked to wait an hour or more. (Emergency care situations would be justified exceptions to the rule.)

All benefit when All are on time.

HAVING IT TOGETHER

So many times we think others have it together...that their lives are without stress, or somehow better than our own.

Then we start talking with them, and find it's not so.

FAD DIETS

Fad diets!

Years ago they said "Don't eat pasta, it will make you fat."

This makes no sense to me. My family has eaten pasta twice a day, every day their entire lives.

If there was a problem with pasta, we'd all be dead.

Then it was potatoes being fattening.

Potatoes are fattening when you put fattening things on them.

We slice the potatoes and cook them in olive oil with spices.

Fad diets are just that.

PICKING A MAN FOR YOUR DAUGHTERS

When my wife and I looked at the men our daughters were dating, to provide input when asked, we looked for certain qualities.

Of course, the girls wanted a man they were attracted to. That made sense, and we looked from the perspective of whether that man would make a good husband, listening not just to what he said, but to how he said it.

We looked for a lot of things: a good sense of humor, a family man and business-oriented, and a happy person people enjoy being with.

It helps if the man is a gentleman in the way he treats others, and has a professional career of some kind or skill with his hands- polite and a good communicator.

If my wife didn't like the young man, she'd say, "I don't think that's the right one for you."

I believe this is something the mother should give input on, and I said very little unless I saw something I didn't like, and then I'd comment very gently.

When my wife said something, she did not say it as criticism. The kids knew she said it because she cared about them, and saw things they did not see.

Because we have close relationships with our kids, they listened.

For the kids, picking their husband or wife was a difficult choice. There are always positives and negatives.

In the end, they ended up listening to our thoughts and made up their own minds and hearts, and all are happily married.

WELL-BEHAVED KIDS

People often tell me and my wife, "You have such well-behaved kids, what's your secret?"

We learned from our parents to respect parents and especially older people, and to listen to the wisdom they have to share.

The way I personally do it, and it's worked great for me, is that kids should be able to have fun and be kids, but then if I say that's enough now, do this- not this, they better listen.

I never have had too much trouble getting them to listen, and only spanked them lightly once.

I let them know where I stand, and after that it's just talking to them to let them know not to do it.

If your reasoning is valid, kids respect your comments.

ALLOWANCE

I've never believed in paying kids to do things to help keep the household going.

I think it sends an inappropriate message of entitlement that can come back to bite both the parents and the kids in years ahead.

My view is: You live here, so you contribute, and if you need something and we can afford it, we'll buy it.

But you will not be "paid" to live here, or "paid" to make a contribution to family.

TALKING WITH OTHER PEOPLE

When I first meet somebody, I'll always try my best to make things easier for the other person.

I try to be easy to get along with, and see how the other person responds.

Yes, people are willing to talk to you.

Treat people well and they open up.

People come to the shop for the first time, and 45 minutes later they have told me their whole life story.

People from all walks of life.

Treat people well, and you'll be amazed at what they'll share with you, and the trust they will show.

THE BEATER

I have never been embarrassed to be seen driving a beat up car or truck.

I used to go to the hair show downtown, where old grain silos were remade into apartments and retail, called Quaker Square.

It was winter time, and we only had one car my wife was driving, and a really rusty pickup truck.

I got dressed up in a 3-piece suit and cashmere coat, and the weather was so bad I told my wife I did not want her to drive me.

I pulled in the parking lot with the rusting, hole-pocked truck, where I saw 4 or 5 of the ladies I worked with.

I blew the horn and blew the horn, but they didn't look.

I saw them inside. "I blew the horn 4 or 5 times, didn't you see me?"

"You didn't drive that thing," they said.

"Yes I did."

WHY MEN WANT YOUNGER WOMEN

I think that psychologically, it makes them feel better.

They want to show off to other people, "See how pretty my wife is!"

It's an ego thing.

Some of them get what they want, the majority of the mixed-age marriages don't last.

THE PRICE OF ITALIAN FASHION

In Italy, most people buy one suit a year which is handmade, and it is in the very latest fashion.

People enjoy wearing the latest look and value quality.

In America, people buy many suits a year, but they are typically not custom or handmade, and not the latest fashion.

I don't know which is better, but they are different.

LEAD THE WAY OVER THE BRIDGE

I always told my kids: There are two ways to be with your friends.

Either you follow your friend over the bridge and let them lead the way, or you lead, and go the way you want.

IN RELATIONSHIPS, LOOK FOR
WHAT YOU CAN GIVE
...NOT WHAT YOU CAN GET

A good question to ask in relationships is, "What do you have to give back?"

Men should ask how they can contribute to the relationship, with a little less emphasis on what they are going to get.

LA FAMIGLIA

THE HAIR STUDIO AT HOME
(As related by Vincenza Cornacchione)

Guido sold his old shop in town, and said he was going to build a new hair salon attached to our home.

I didn't understand why he wanted to do that.

Then I understood.

He saw the kids in the morning before they went to school, and all day on weekends, and when they got home from school.

He'd take breaks and play games with them.

At night, he'd go in their rooms to see they were asleep.

"I'm going to stay close to the family," he said. And he did.

I can't tell you how many women have said how much they wish their husbands had done the same.

All our kids grew up fine. All are happy with families, and all are successful.

Guido was right.

SEAGULLS AND STARS
(As related by Vincenza Cornacchione)

One time, Guido painted the kitchen light yellow and he painted the ceiling blue.

It was so strange to see, I lay awake at night wondering what he was thinking.

He said, "I'm going to paint stars."

I didn't understand that either.

Then I saw him with paper cutouts of seagulls and stars. He laid the template on the ceiling, and sprayed with color.

"There are too many seagulls and stars," I told him the next day.

"No, that's the way it's supposed to be."

Then people started coming over and they all said the same thing... they loved it!

That's Guido.

OUR HOME
(As related by Vincenza Cornacchione)

The first time I saw our current home, I couldn't wait to get off the property.

The grass was so high, you couldn't walk.

"Oh, this house has potential," Guido said, "I'm going to put the hair salon right next to the house so I can enjoy the kids and you every day."

First, he planted the grapevine, before we even bought the house.

"I want a grapevine and it has to go in now to grow."

We bought the house, and he would tear it up while I was gone at work.

I'd come home and the walls would be torn down.

"What are you doing?"

"The walls are in the wrong place," he said.

But then, when he finished, it made sense what he was doing.

Then I went to Italy for a month, and when I returned he was hesitant to take me home.

We did a few errands, and when we got home his brother was putting the finishing touches on a new bathroom.

What a surprise!

Guido, he's like that.

VINCENZA ON RAISING CHILDREN
(As related by Vincenza Cornacchione)

Is it hard to raise children in America? I don't know, it is a different atmosphere from where I grew up.

Certainly faster-paced, with less respect for elders.

Being a mother requires different techniques and psychology for each child.

You can talk to one child sweetly, quietly, they may be very sensitive, but for another stronger-willed child, you have to be more strict.

I always tried to find a way to say what I needed to say without getting the child upset.

You have to put more time in with some to get a positive result.

My children are all different. Emilio and Rita are more outgoing, more outspoken. They can do anything with anyone. But Lisa and Carlo are more conservative, they pick the people who they are with more carefully.

I referred many things to Guido, "Let's see what your father says."

Whatever he said, I would agree.

And they did not lie, because they knew that sooner or later, I would get to the truth.

The hardest thing about being a parent is the responsibility. You always want to be the best mother you can be, and care the best you can for your children.

It's not always immediately clear how to do that.

Guido and I, we tried together always, and it's worked out.

TIN-SLICED
(As related by Lisa Cornacchione Jeras)

My sister, Rita and I were no strangers to grocery shopping when we were young. It was part of our weekly routine with Mamma who insisted on the freshest ingredients, at least those that came from outside of our family garden. The delicatessen became our favorite pitstop of the entire fieldtrip. While Mamma would say, "I wanna pound of salami tin-sliced," Rita and I would enjoy free samples that the deli worker so kindly gave to us.

Many years passed and Rita and I found ourselves at a different delicatessen ordering our own salami. This time Mamma was not with us. We were off at college, roommates taking our own fieldtrip to the grocers. Independent and proud, we walked up to the delicounter and ordered, "We would like a pound of salami tin-sliced please." The deli worker stopped for a moment and questioned us, "How would you like that sliced?"

Nervously, we replied just as Mamma always had, "Tin-sliced." Bewildered, the deliworker questioned us, "You mean thin-sliced, ...right?"

Could it be that after all these years, that what Rita and I had interpreted as deli talk ("tin-sliced") was really just Mamma's Italian accent shining thru!

In a panic, we dialed Mamma from the store. "Mamma," I asked, "You know when we would go to the store and you would order salami tin-sliced...what did you mean by tin-sliced?"

She responded, "tin," as if she had not understood the question.

"No," I pressed, "What did you mean by tin? Is that deli-talk?"

Mamma, somewhat confused, responded again, "I mean tin, not tick."

At that moment, we realized Italians have difficulty pronouncing the "th" sound.

We starting ordering thin-sliced cuts after that.

MY MAMMA AND PAPA
(As related by Lisa Cornacchione Jeras)

My mamma and papa are very different. Mamma is more reserved and quiet, and she's really concerned about what people think.

My papa is more free-spirited and creative. As long as he likes it, he doesn't care about what other people think.

My sister and I grew up being told by our parents that they loved us.

Few of our friends had that, and we were surprised when our friends told us this.

My mamma and papa touch my heart.

FRIENDS TO KEEP- AND FRIENDS TO AVOID

You meet people all the time and then you pretty much figure out that this person will become a friend you can keep, or because of their personality or what they say or don't say, do or don't do, decide you don't want to be close friends. It's a natural healthy process of selection.

Therefore I don't spend too much time with the ones I don't think are the types I want to be close friends with.

In a tactful way, I avoid getting together with those people.

I've had people ask me to go to lunch, or to go shoot guns. One kept offering different days, and I just said "No."

I believe it's not a good thing to spend too much time with people that are going in a different direction than I like in life.

So I search out those which are.

What criteria do I apply?

I select people who don't smoke or drink too much, who don't use drugs, and who seldom speak negatively of others, those which mistreat their girlfriends or wives, and gossips.

One thing I'm concerned about is that bad behaviors may rub off on me- best to be selective.

I especially like those which are positive, happy, respectful, and have a good sense of humor.

It's the same with kids. I've found that whatever the parents' attitudes and mannerisms are, it kind of filters into the kids.

When my kids brought home a friend, I was interested to learn and know about their friends and parents- who they are and the lifestyle they live. The answers become the basis for how I feel my kids might be impacted by being with those kids too frequently.

If I didn't like what I saw, I politely explained to my child that I didn't want them to spend too much time with that individual, and then explain why. I always provide my children with reasons for what I do.

THE BOBCAT
(As communicated by Emilio Cornacchione)

About ten years ago, when Carlo moved out of the house, my papa adopted a new son, a small Bobcat earthmover.

My brother, Carlo was really complaining to me about it.

"Why did he buy it now instead of when we were kids and were moving everything like stones and earth?"

He asked Papa, and Papa answered, "How do you think I kept you out of trouble?"

We often worked 4 hours a day around the house.

If we came home from school tired, we did not take a nap because Mamma and Papa were always working in the yard or on projects. How could we think about lying down when we were so much younger than they?

Once I did take a nap, but I got up quickly and put my clothes on to help them.

They never said, "Hey, what are you doing laying down?"

JOBS FROM MY FATHER
(As related by Carlo Cornacchione)

My father had jobs that my brother and I had to do every day when we were growing up.

At a young age, we learned many tasks such as painting, stucco, carpentry, landscaping, tree pruning, digging, edging, lawn mowing, planting a garden, and more.

At the time my brother and I were not too fond of the whole process, although there were some great moments. Sometimes Papa would have Mamma make a pitcher of high balls (seven and seven) and we would be allowed to have some after a hard days work. Papa would say "If you work like a man, then you are allowed to drink like a man."

Later on in life I found that I already knew how to do many things because of what my father had taught my brother and me. In fact when I purchased my first home, a two unit multi-family property, at the age of 22, I was amazed at all of the things that I could do on my own.

I saved a tremendous amount of money, which I really did not have a lot of at the time, and got great satisfaction upon completion of each project. I patched walls, textured ceilings, painted rooms, made plumbing and electrical upgrades, installed a new front lawn, and landscaped the whole property from front to back. The neighbors who varied in age were all stopping over to compliment my work and tell me how good it looked.

I definitely learned the value of working hard and how it can transform your life into one of pride and success.

BROKEN GLASS
(As related by Vincenza Cornacchione)

One day I came in the living room to find Guido breaking up a glass mirror.

"Why are you breaking the glass in the living room?," I asked.

"I'm going to glue the broken pieces to the wall and cover the edges."

I thought he was kidding.

The next day the glass pieces were on the wall, like he'd pushed them into the wall.

Everyone loves it.

I've become accustomed to coming home and seeing something in pieces, walls missing, and the like. He does it quickly, like a little boy would do so as not to get caught.

I never know what he's going to do, but I have to admit it always seems to work well.

WHY GO TO BARS WHEN YOU CAN ENJOY FRIENDS AT HOME?

Why go to a bar and spend money, when you can create your own group, and be in the safety of your home?

This relates to how to protect your kids.

After one New Years Eve party at my home where we had over 110 guests, my son Emilio said he was going to a bar with friends.

I explained, "There's a full bar downstairs and all the food you could want to eat. The point I'm trying to make is that you've all been drinking and you'll be at risk driving, and at risk from others on the road."

I'm not cheap, but one does have to ask, "What are you looking for?"

Before Carlo was married, he also wanted to go out late after our home parties, and I said, "2:30 in the morning is not a time to look for a woman to date."

They learned from the above and told me years later, "You were right."

THE RESPONSIBILITY FOR COLLEGE WAS MINE
(As related by Carlo Cornacchione)

Thinking back to when I was a sophomore in high school, I remember my papa telling me that he and Mamma were not going to be able to provide me money for college, and that I needed to start thinking about what I wanted to do in life and how I was going to achieve it.

I ended up going to vocational through a program at the high school to learn Cosmetology so I could work with my papa and brother. I finished the program and got my license, but felt that it was not for me.

Then I joined the Naval Reserves and signed up for RAMP (Rapid Allied Medical Program), which was an eight-year enlistment in which I would get monies for a two-year college medical laboratory degree.

I went back to school and completed a bachelor's degree in Health Arts and a master's degree in Health Services Administration.

SAUSAGE

In winter, just after Christmas, we would slaughter a pig.

To make the sausage, we'd use mostly meat and a little fat.

Everything was ground up, and we mixed in spices like black pepper, red pepper, and salt.

Then we'd use a funnel to squeeze the mixture into a casing made of pig intestines about an inch and-a-half thick, and 5 feet long.

Punching any air pockets with a needle kept the sausage from molding.

To dry the sausage, we'd hang it over a pipe and rotate it every day or so, so the part hanging over the pipe dried too.

The sausage was cut into 5" pieces and put in a clay pot, and filled with melted lard (lard being the fat tissue seen on bacon).

This preserved the sausage, and when we made dinner we'd scrape out the needed number of pieces and melt off the lard in a pan, preparing the sausage to be heated for dinner later that evening. We used the lard for cooking as one would use olive oil.

With no phone or cell phone, we didn't know if we'd have guests for dinner, or not. And the rule was that if a guest came, you might be the one who gave them your sausage.

That night, we all had the one piece of sausage on our plate, but my cousin waited to eat it last, which was his custom.

In came the roof repairman, and my mother asked if he'd like something to eat.

"Yes, I would thank you."

My cousin grabbed the sausage off his plate and held it behind his back, so my mother would think he already ate it.

The dog pushed in through the door behind the repairman, grabbed the sausage from my cousin and ran out.

My cousin ran after him, yelling, "Give me back my sausage," but he never saw that sausage again.

HARD WORK
(As related by Carlo Cornacchione)

Hard work has been a way of life for me as learned from my Papa. I worked for many of my papa's clients when I was little, doing miscellaneous jobs for five dollars an hour.

In high school I delivered pizza for two years and saved enough money to put a down payment on my first home.

My brother and I saved money to purchase our own vehicles, which Papa helped us to find. And we paid for our own insurance and gas... something you don't see often in today's society.

Children are just given everything, and they don't value and appreciate what they have, or feel that they should have to work for anything.

HIDING FROM MY FATHER
(As related by Carlo Cornacchione)

My family was coming home from a vacation at Niagara Falls in our motor home. We arrived at home around two in the morning.

Needless to say, I was very tired, even though I was not the one that had to drive. Papa wanted the whole family to help unload everything from the motor home that night.

Well, I was really tired and did not want to do that, so I went into the house and hid behind the couch. I was going to just sleep there, but Papa kept calling for me to help.

I did not respond.

Eventually Papa found me and I was in big trouble. I ran out the front door and around the city block with Papa hot on my trail.

Papa was fairly fast for his age, but I was much faster. As I was quite a bit ahead of my father, I had enough time to find a good hiding place around the next door neighbor's wagon, which was parked in his driveway with a lot of stuff on and around it. Papa and my brother looked for me for about one and a half hours.

They were just about to give up when my brother spotted me. I shook my head frantically for him not to tell Papa, but he just got a big smile on his face and revealed where I was hiding. I really paid the price for that stunt.

I did learn a valuable lesson. I should have just helped and done the work instead of avoiding the work, and wasting time and getting into trouble.

CATHY'S BRIDAL SHOWER
(As related by Catherine Cornacchione, Carlo's wife)

For my bridal shower, Mamma and Papa threw the most beautiful and elaborate shower possible for Carlo and me. It was more beautiful than I could ever have dreamed!

They planned and made everything homemade from the menu to the decorations. Mamma and Papa made wedding soup with pastina, chicken breast with cream sauce, green beans almondine, salad, homemade bread, homemade wine, cookies, cake, and desserts.

Papa and 10 men in the family, including cousins, and uncles, served all the women our food wearing red bow ties and red cummerbunds (our wedding color), Mamma had made by hand.

She also made several heart pillows and baskets with white satin material with sprays of pearls and doves attached, and a white tree with dove birds that was the centerpiece on the cake table. All the tables were covered in fine white linens, with red cloth napkins, and red and white rose bouquets.

They made banners which hung around the room saying, "Two hearts soon to be one...Cathy & Carlo," and another saying "Buon Appetito and Best Wishes." They also made a large grapevine wreath with letters spelling "Cathy & Carlo," with doves and flowers around the wreath, with our picture in the center.

They put their heart and soul into every fine detail of our shower, and it was so beautiful.

It was apparent to me from the first time that I met Papa and Mamma, that this is how they operate in all aspects of their lives, from how they raised their children with upstanding morals and values, to how they work their jobs and keep their special Cornacchione home.

It is all their heart and soul, 100 percent, and I love that!

PAPA TOLD US THE TRUTH ABOUT COLLEGE EDUCATION
(As related by Emilio Cornacchione)

All our friends had families which could afford to send their kids to college.

Papa told each of us about our Junior year in high school, "I'll help you how I can, but I have taken you this far, you have to take it from here. You can get a college education by going into the Army, or Navy, get a sports scholarship, or an academic scholarship."

I had to think about what to do.

Imagine being a parent and saying to your child, "This is as far as we can take you, but you have all these options ahead of you, and you can do it."

We were forced to take responsibility for a big decision, think it through, and have the perseverance to see it through.

Going to school was "ours;" we made the decision, and we paid, or joined the military or got loans or scholarships.

So many other kids didn't apply themselves in school. It was paid by mom and dad and they looked at it like an obligation.

To think that my father had the fortitude to say this not just once, but to each of the four children is amazing.

All of us worked it out. All of us are successful in our areas.

EMILIO AND WORKING THE SOIL
(As related by Emilio Cornacchione)

My brother and I were both good baseball players, so the kids wanted us to play with them.

But they had no chores- while we were working the soil in our garden, which was backbreaking work.

They said, "Why do you have to do all that work? We don't."

We thought it would go faster if they helped us, but after three hours they said, "We quit, we're going home, call us when you're done."

Working in the garden taught us how to work the soil with the minimum of effort, and to put family responsibilities before play.

NEW YEAR'S EVE
(By Lisa Cornacchione Jeras)

(Author's note: Of all the stories of Guido and his family, this seems to reflect the family atmosphere of love and fun best. Enjoy!)

Food...check. Guest list...check. Music...check. This is the list of things Rita and I would review every year while preparing for the big bash.

It was a family tradition dating back to before we were even born, but it's the only way we knew how to celebrate New Year's Eve.

Food, family, friends, and fun. These were the ingredients for a party...Cornacchione style. We seemed to have them all, but they came with a dutiful price to prepare for the big event.

We would spend hours preparing, mostly in the few days before the big date.

Most people when hosting an annual event probably have a set routine- clean the house, set the decorations, and prepare or order a set menu. Not us. The cleaning the house part was always a magnified task due to Papa's never-ending housing projects.

Missing walls, unfinished floors, and endless construction dust created a messy recipe for cleaning. The one year we hauled loads and loads of lumber, scraps, etc., out of a newly built indoor bocci court measuring 12 feet by 60 feet! What a job that was! I can remember thinking along with my other siblings, "Why do we have to do all this work? Why can't we just go to one of our friends' houses for New Year's Eve for once?"

Next came the decorations and music. Since many parts of the house were often unfinished, we used a staple gun to hang balloons and streamers. Papa had bought a disco ball one year from a junk store, which he mounted in the center of our family room, several years back, yet that disco ball has been there all year-round ever since.

Mamma purchased over 30 sombreros from a Mexican restaurant going out of business one year which are still to this day brought out just before midnight and passed around to all the guests. Our homemade DJ booth also required quite a bit of preparation.

Mamma had a special array of hits that had to be played at midnight in the perfect order. First was *Celebration* by Kool and the Gang, followed by *We are Family* by the Pointer Sisters, and then *Party All the Time* by Eddie Murphy.

Every year when Papa would think of a way to construct a DJ station, you could always hear Mamma saying, "I wanna my songs ready!" And, we can't forget the Broom Dance Medley- that was a favorite. Men and women would pair up in couples around the dance floor.

One man would stand in the middle of the couples with a broom. The Italian songs would play and the couples start dancing. Once the man dancing with the broom would drop the broom, the couples would have to switch partners, kind of like musical chairs. The man left without a woman would have to dance with the broom and so on.

In 1998, our wishes had finally been granted (or so we thought). We decided to take the year off from doing the party at our house. This meant we were able to do what we had so longed for....experience New Year's Eve someplace else. Our plans were set. Rita and I were to attend a festive party in downtown Cleveland where our friend from college was to receive a surprise wedding proposal from her boyfriend at the stroke of midnight! Her boyfriend had invited us and other close friends to witness and share in the momentous event. Emilio had other ideas that were sure to involve girls, and Carlo and Cathy had plans of their own. Dressed up and full of excitement, Rita and I headed downtown.

As we entered the party venue we could not believe our eyes. Beautiful flower centerpieces on the tables, sparkling lights, and gorgeous decorations filled the ballroom, not like the homemade things we put up every year. It just felt so pretty and fancy!

We couldn't wait to see what happened at the stroke of midnight! The moment finally came. Five, four, three, two, one...."Happy New Year," everyone shouted as our friend knelt down on one knee and proposed to his astonished girlfriend. It was perfect. Everyone hugging one another and congratulating the happy, newly-engaged couple.

Yet, something was missing, an emptiness that couldn't be filled. No *Celebration* could be heard playing, no sombreros, no disco ball turning, no tradition. We kept wondering what Papa and Mamma were doing and where were Emilio and Carlo? Where were all the cousins?

Suddenly, a flood of phone calls came over our mobile phones. It was practically every family member we knew wishing each other tidings of joy and love! We all longed to be together just as we always had done.....how IRONIC!

Well, since that year, the annual party continues- going on 47 years strong, minus a few years for sicknesses and travel! Those homemade decorations get more creative each year. That disco ball is still hanging in Papa and Mamma's house. And the bocci court that was such a pain... that has been our annual eating area set for 70- 80 people ever since. I guess some traditions never grow old.

GUIDO'S LOVE TRULY SAVED OUR BUSINESS
(As related by Emilio Cornacchione and Gino Chiodo)

After years of styling hair and putting on training seminars nation-wide for international product manufacturers, my business partner who I consider a brother, Gino, and I started a new hair salon in Pittsburgh.

It was the culmination of a decade of dreams and hard work, and was right downtown with chairs for 20 stylists. With that big space came big overhead.

"We put in every dime we had of cash, mortgaged homes, and maxed out every credit card...I mean, we were fully exposed," said Gino, who had recently married and had a first child on the way.

A competitor who we'd worked for previously (who had filed for bankruptcy protection), hired a law firm to get a restraining order to stop the two of us from styling our customers' hair, claiming we had violated a mythical non-compete agreement.

But there was no non-compete agreement, it was a false allegation. But we still had to hire a lawyer.

"And their timing? They served us the papers just days after we opened- and there we stood, over our head in bills, with no ability to generate funds," said Gino.

After exhausting all of our options and financial resources, we were on the verge of bankruptcy. Our only other option was to ask our family for help.

We went to Papa and told him about our situation. He embraced our challenge as if it were his own, listened to our issues and reassured us that everything was going to work out.

He talked with his brother Leo, and Uncle Leo and Aunt Concetta lent us $100,000 to cover the biggest roadblocks any start-up company could ever face... legal fees to fight a suit, and monies needed for startup operations, with Guido guaranteeing the loan.

We prevailed in court and our business journey continues thanks to family!

A leading newspaper writer picked up the story and told the public what was going on, and we posted huge letters in all the store windows prior to the court date explaining the injustice," said Gino.

"We got huge press, all of it favorable, and this helped build the business," said Gino. "We now have 2 Hair Salons & Spas employing about 80 people with a third on the way, and a fast-growing hair care product company."

"If it had not been for my father, and his Uncle Leo & Aunt Concetta, we'd have been fed to the lions," said Emilio. (Note Emilio and Gino paid back the loan in full, with interest.)

You can find yourself in a situation where your only protection is your family's love, where they are the sole force between you and personal tragedy.

In my hour of need, my family was there.

Thank you Papa.

Emilio (your son) and Gino (Cumpare & adopted son)

WHO IS MY HERO?

Sometimes in a family, one spouse claims the other is having an affair, and we find out they both were.

When kids get into trouble, many think it's the kid's fault.

99% of the time it starts with the parents.

Kids see what you do, not what you say.

So, who is the hero when the parents let you down?

GIOVANNI...IL MIGLIORE VINO
(As related by Guido Cornacchione)

In Italy, we call the best homemade wine from the household in that year, "Il Migliore Vino."

Giovanni was not related to my family in any way, but he came from the same small town in Southern Italy I did, Fossalto.

As he had worked with his father who was an electrician, he was skilled at working with his hands.

In 2003, Giovanni and two others from Fossalto, Italy, came to visit the United States, and they all stayed at our home.

I was working late that night getting the house ready for our annual New Year's Eve party, just two days away.

My daughters and sons and guests came in about midnight, and they asked if they could help. I said, "No, it's pretty late, I'm almost done. I'll finish up."

Giovanni walked over to me. He did not ask if I needed any help, but said, "Just tell me what you want done."

I asked him to paint the wood around the bocci court and he had it done in 45 minutes.

He did a good job and was willing to work.

If my kids didn't have other company to take care of and entertain, they'd have helped.

The visitors from Fossalto had 30 day visas, after which they planned to return to Italy.

Giovanni told my kids he'd like to stay in America, and found he was able to extend his visa to 3 months.

"You're welcome to stay here at our home, and I'll get you little jobs here and there. You can use my car to go to school to learn English."

He said "Great."

At the time I was creating an apartment on a property I owned, and he helped in many ways, and went to school to learn English.

After 3 months he went back to Italy, and then again came to visit us for 3 more months.

My daughter Rita and he were attracted to each other, and started spending more time together. He continued to go to school, and they started dating. He was living with us, and in some ways already a part of the family.

They extended his visa for one more year, and he and Rita got engaged and then married.

I talked with a client who owned businesses about a job for Giovanni, and while he did not have a job opening, a neighbor of his did.

"Oh no," said the owner of the business when my client spoke with him about Giovanni, "I don't want foreigners working for me. I've had them, and they don't work out."

My client said, "You should give this guy a try."

"Ok, we'll give this guy a try."

A few months later the business owner came to my salon with a gift.

"This kid is the best I've ever seen, I just wanted to come and thank you."

Today, Giovanni is Vice President of the company and travels throughout the world on their behalf.

He's been a great husband to my daughter Rita, and a welcome addition to our family.

Growing up on a farm, I recognize and respect, "Il Migliore Vino."

PHOTOGRAPHS

Photo of Fossalto, Italy, home of Guido as a child

Oil painting of Guido Cornacchione in his 30's

Guido at age 22, taken in Fossalto, Italy

Vincenza in high school, taken in Sicily

*Wedding photo of Vincenza and
Guido Cornacchione*

*Guido age 20 on the family farm in Fossalto,
Italy, washing clothes with family*

Nicoletta and Emilio Cornacchione,
mamma and papa of Guido

Guido's father, Emilio, on a horse on the family farm in Fossalto, Italy

The schoolhouse Guido attended in the town of Fossalto, Italy

Guido in England, age 24, standing with his cousins, just before he came to America

Guido's cousin, Carmine, walking the former family farm in Fossalto, Italy

The former family farm in Fossalto, Italy

Nicoletta Cornacchione, Guido's mother

Guido as an adult at a farmhouse in the town of
Fossalto, Italy

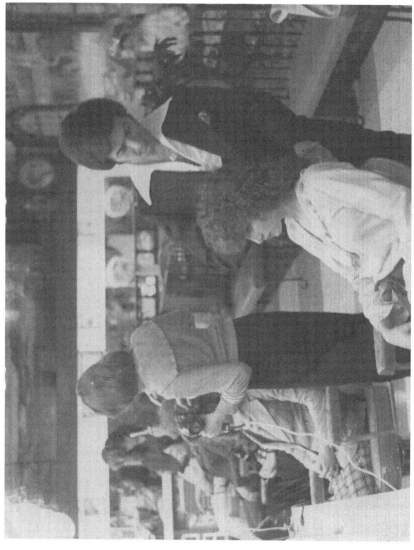

Photo of Mr. Guido and client at his first hair salon with 9 stations, before hair studio moved to home annex

Photo of Mr. Guido and client at his first hair salon in Akron with 9 stations, before hair studio moved to home annex

Circular montage of various photos of
Mr. Guido, hair stylist

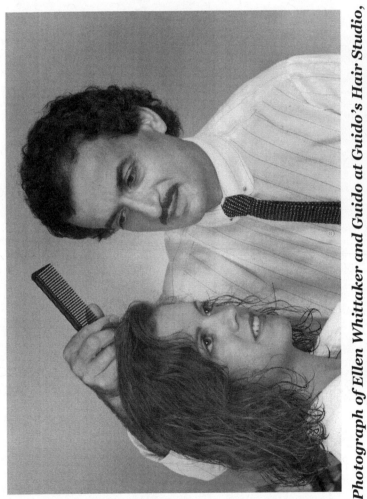

Photograph of Ellen Whittaker and Guido at Guido's Hair Studio, annexed to their home in Ohio. This photo was used on Guido's business cards and mailbox for many years.

Photograph of Ellen Whittaker and Guido at Guido's Hair Studio. Ellen was a friend of Guido's Love author, David Kettlewell, and of Kim Henderson, who shot the photo.

Guido with his first son, Emilio, age 2 months

Guido Cornacchione with his first son, Emilio.

Guido in his custom made sport coat,
Fossalto, Italy, age 24

Vincenza, Carlo, Rita, Emilio, Guido and Lisa (left to right)

*Guido Cornacchione with his grandson by
Lisa, Mariano*

Guido's children as adults; Rita, Lisa, Emilio, Carlo

Guido and Vincenza surrounded by Rita, Lisa w. Mariano,
Emilio, and Carlo (clockwise from lower left)

Vincenza and Guido Cornacchione

Guido with some of his grandsons

Guido playing bocci on one of the outdoor courts at his home in Ohio

Vincenza and Guido at their wedding,
on left are her relatives, to right are his

Lisa (Cornacchione) Jeras and Vjeko Jeras, at their wedding, under tree, (Lisa is Guido's daughter)

*Carlo (Guido's son) and Cathy Cornacchione
at their wedding*

Donina and Emilio Cornacchione (Guido's son) in limousine at their wedding

*Guido and Vincenza, with Vincenza's
two brothers and their wives*

Guido's daughter, Rita (Cornacchione) Brienza and Giovanni Brienza at their wedding.

*Guido (second from far right) and
his brothers and sisters.*

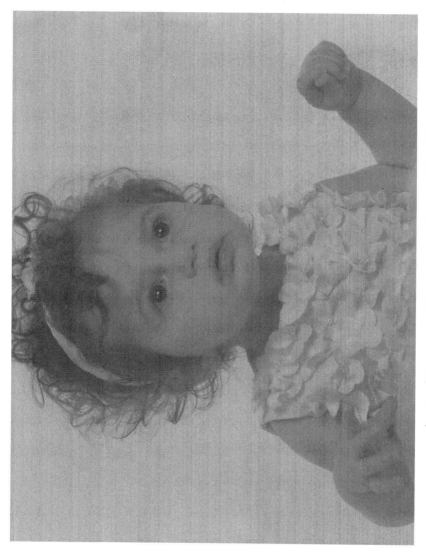

Aria Emi Cornacchione, daughter of Emilio and Donina, (Guido's grandchild)

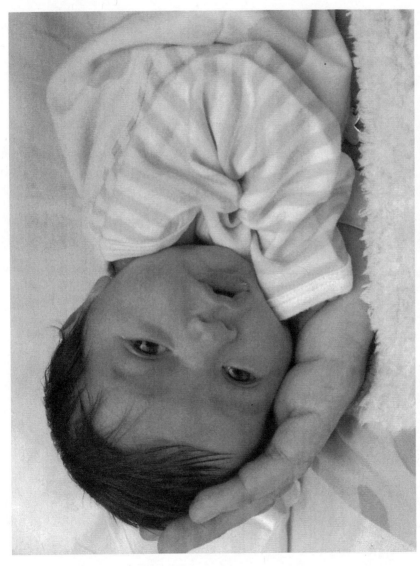

Enzo Emilio Cornacchione, Emilio's second child, grandchild to Guido

Guido and his wife, Vincenza

HAIR CARE

BIGGEST MISTAKES IN HAIR CARE

The biggest mistakes made by hair stylists are due to communication...actually, the lack of it.

Talk with your stylist about what you want, every time you visit.

Stylists start to cut the client's hair without clarity on what they want to achieve.

Stylists need to take time to discuss colors in detail with you. When a client says they want a color, the stylist needs to discuss the various shades in detail, and use hair samples to show the exact color, holding them up to the client's hair.

I am the creator and the artist, and the communication must take place between me and the client.

You see a lot of people take things for granted.

Perhaps their clients have been coming to them for a long time, and the time may not be spent really thinking things through.

If your hairstylist takes things for granted, it's time to find a new stylist.

BLOWDRYING...MORE THAN MEETS THE EYE

When drying hair, I only use the towel to blot off excess water, and I never rub or smush the hair.

Hair is a fibre and when you crush it together, it roughens the hair and makes it frizzy.

I may blot the hair with a towel to remove water, but no smushing!

Point the dryer into the hair at least eight inches away.

Keep the dryer moving, and use the lower heat setting. It's better for the hair.

Try not to point the hair dryer directly at the scalp.

The dryer should blow on the hair only, with the hair held by a comb or brush.

HAIR CARE PRODUCTS...STAY WITH A WINNER

The longer I care for hair, the more I see that it's totally unique to each woman, and a very individual thing.

Your hair may be oily or dry.

Pick a product suitable for your type of hair, ask your hairstylist's advice, and once you have a product grouping which is working for you...stick with it.

HAIR CARE...THE LOOK YOU LIKE, THE LOOK YOU WANT

For a woman, the choice of look for her hair is the most important aspect of her presentation to the world...the foundation of her look in every sense of the word.

It is the basis for how she feels each day, an expression of her spirit, her femininity, her sexuality, and the single common denominator of fashion for her presentation to the world.

Clothes can be changed or given away, but your hair is with you always, and being on the uppermost or highest part of your body- and on the same level as eyes looking at you- it is noticed!

Some men have trouble relating with that. They grump about the time a woman spends caring for her hair, pacing up and down and muttering to themselves.

Men need to understand the importance women give to their hair, and "get it."

One place to start in selecting your hairstyle is to evaluate the kind of work you do...what will fit into your lifestyle or profession? Here is an area your hairstylist can help with.

If you wear a suit, updating with a new hairstyle makes sense. It's all part of your look and presentation.

Pick a hairstyle which you feel is the right one for your lifestyle- take into account things like whether you have to interact with a phone all day.

Will you be outside in the wind? Can you do what you need to do easily, without affecting the look of your hairstyle?

The amount of daily care required is also high on a woman's list of concerns relating to her hair.

It can be confusing, because a style which looks great in a photo on one woman, say in a magazine, may not work for you. Sometimes a woman decides to wear a hairstyle not perfectly suited to her, other times a woman stays closer to her safety zone.

Hair type lends itself to specific styles.

With hair styling, change is good.

A change in hairstyle is always noticed by so many people. "Oh, this is better than what you've been wearing. Yes, I like this on you, or, I can't really say."

Better or worse, change in hairstyle is *always* noticed.

And it's just as important for men as it is for women.

Men want to look their best for their wife, or should. (Many men need to consider this.)

Some men, they think as long as their wife looks nice, he does not have to.

It's better if both of them look their best.

HEALTHY HAIR, DIET & MEDICAL CONDITIONS

Hair is a fibre, it grows out almost like a plant, and cutting the hair does not hurt it.

Hair looks best when your nutrition is optimal.

The root of the hair gets nutrition from the scalp, which then feeds the rest of the hair.

Loss of hair is often genetic.

There are 7 layers of skin, and the root is under the first layer, so hair grows through layers of skin and comes out the scalp.

Hair grows out of what you can picture is a straw, or tube.

At a certain point, the hair picks up color as it passes a given point in the tube.

It's harder for the hair to grow through the scalp as we age, because the tube constricts.

Billions are spent on hair care to encourage the tube to reopen so the hair can grow.

You can tell when you look at hair whether the individual has a good diet.

Eating disorders damage hair, and medications often affect the results of a perm.

In general, if you want healthy hair, eat a healthful diet.

BUYING NEW HAIR CARE PRODUCTS

I am not against trying new things, but just because something is new, or costs more, does not necessarily mean it's better.

The promises from manufacturers are many, and unending.

They promise your hair will feel softer, that it will curl better, or that the shampoo is the perfect choice for curl.

From my years of experience, many of these promises are not so.

I stick with good products when they work.

TRENDY

Be discerning when it comes to following trends.

I'm all for keeping up with the latest trends, but be smart enough to not get caught up in a trend when it's doesn't look good on you.

I remember when tights came in, some looked great in them and some did not.

You want to enjoy trends and be trendy, but not when it looks bad.

HAIR NEEDS TO CHANGE WITH AGE

How you wear your hair needs to change with age.

Between the ages of twenty and thirty, there is little change.

Between thirty and forty, a bit more.

More between forty and fifty.

Longer hair is often worn by young women, and shorter hair more common after age 35.

Color of hair also changes with age. You can start to include gray, or not.

People color their hair for many reasons, some like a given color and others want to look younger.

BEAUTY

The beginning of a woman's beauty is her perception of her own beauty.

When a woman has an internal confidence and knowledge of what looks good on her, men often perceive that as beauty.

(Men may put on a suit and just know it "looks right." It's the same thing).

Beauty is not always the beautiful face and fine figure.

I look at the whole package, the entire person.

Do they smile, do they look happy, do they walk with their head up?

A conversation quickly tells me where they stand.

I see what I see, but I always listen.

If I like what I hear, then I start to see more, and a woman becomes beautiful.

HAIR COLOR BASICS

It is very difficult for an amateur to get good results with coloring hair.

This is because there are issues with coloring most people don't understand.

How to manage coloring changes depending on what you're trying to achieve.

Say you have dark brown hair and want to be blonde.

If you apply a blonde shade color directly to dark brown hair, it comes out red or orange.

Coloring to blonde is a two step process: first you extract the dark color pigment already in the hair, and then apply the lighter blonde color.

A developer (such as peroxide), is used to open the cuticle of hair and remove existing color. Then the new coloring is applied, but it has to be the exact amount to get to the new color you desire, and manufacturers' products work differently with various types of hair.

Hair stylists use a system to calculate exactly how much color comes out, and how much goes back in. Colors are actually often a mix of colors. You can also add complexity to hair color by coloring some strands differently than others, called highlighting.

The feel of your hair can be affected by coloring.

The more extraction of color, the more *possibility* there is for hair to feel dry.

I often describe hair as a straw. When you remove its color, it can become a bit more fragile, especially if errors are made. The bleaching takes from 15 minutes to 45 minutes.

Many factors affect the coloring process: starting and end-color desired, damage done from previous work by amateurs, past color changes, type of hair, perms, and general health.

Professionals take into consideration all the factors. I personally feel that success in reaching the perfect color is a bit of an art.

Many who believe that anyone can achieve quality results with coloring hair at home, come to find it's not so.

PASSING AWAY

One day I was running a busy schedule with no lunch break, and all of a sudden the desk girl, Jean, shouts, "Hey Guido, Mary's sister called and said that Mary passed away."

"Does she want to reschedule?," I asked.

Laughter filled the salon.

I had no idea what the American phrase, "passed away," meant.

PERMS

As a fashion trend, perms tend to come and go- as most things relating to fashion do.

When it's here, enjoy it- when not, it will soon be back.

There are many reasons why clients love perms. Because it's a fashion statement, a perm gives you a different look. A woman with straight hair can enjoy a light wave, or more curl.

Perms also make hair behave, and greatly assist in maintaining certain hairstyles.

Permed hair is, as the name implies, more "permanent," far beyond what you can accomplish with a curling iron.

With a tight curl, a perm gives you a fluffier, softer look.

Permed hair feels thicker and more luxurious to the touch, and a little shot of misty water revives them quickly.

Medications taken, and coloring (past and present), both have an effect on perms, and managing all is the greater part of the art of the hair stylist.

When you want to do both color and perm, you always start with the color.

If coloring roots, color the virgin hair and the hair already colored first, then perm.

Incorrectly done, perms often make hair look frizzy. Most of the time that's due to using too small a rod to shape the hair.

Perming solutions break down the hair cuticle, and make the hair more pliable.

In this state it can be easily reshaped with rods of various sizes, and then returned to its natural firmer state with neutralizer.

I always treat hair gently when perming- blotting hair a bit to remove excess moisture after washing out perming solution.

Styling is a major part of the final look of a perm, as you create a new shape for the curls.

Facial shape and body build help to guide the stylist's recommendation on what style to select.

There are a few minor downsides to a perm.

The hair will always be a bit more porous than normal after a perm, and more susceptible to dust and dirt, sunlight and chlorine, from say, a pool.

Perms last many months, so you'll likely have several cuts before you need another.

Perms continue to come into style for all the above reasons, most important being you can enjoy a radically new look *immediately*, making a memorable and noticeable fashion statement.

(Men get perms too, but it's less common.)

EXCEPTIONAL SERVICE TO CUSTOMERS PAYS

When I graduated from beauty school, I got a job in Akron, Ohio, at Polsky's Beauty Salon, which was managed by a huge national franchise organization with 600+ salons, S&L out of New York City.

After 6 months with the company, the Manager asked if I'd like to do a promotion in Cleveland at a major department store, to be a guest stylist for one week.

"I don't think so," I said. "I've only been styling hair for 6 months, and I don't want other stylists to think I know more than they do."

The manager said, "Why don't you think about it tonight, and I'll talk to you tomorrow."

The next morning she approached me again, "*You know* you've been in the business for 6 months, and *I know* you've been in the business for 6 months, but they don't know, and if we don't tell them they will not know."

It became a big success. I'd stand with the stylist for a few minutes and suggest a cut, or a perm, and then the stylist would execute it, and I'd come back to see how it was going, and maybe make a minor change or two.

The female employees working in the department store (there were hundreds), had their hair done, and word traveled quickly.

Women saw the styles and liked them, so, soon it was "Mr. Guido is here from Italy."

More and more people came, and it went so well they asked me to come once a month.

Then they started advertising that I was coming to Cleveland, and they offered a special.

I liked it because there were two of us providing advice (me and the hair stylist), and I enjoyed seeing the women try new looks. Of course, the customers enjoyed it too.

Women tried highlights and offset cuts (shorter on one side than the other), and perms they'd never tried before. We worked together to show them new possibilities.

My boss in Akron, Ohio, was thrilled with all the good things she'd heard from the New York office.

One day I learned how I came to the company's attention.

They tracked their new clients and I had 50 clients, and all became repeat customers. "Everybody stayed with him," my manager reported.

It pays to provide exceptional service.

A GENTLE START

With a new customer, when I see their body is tense, I just talk with them.

I tell them we do not have to do their hair today, we just talk and make it easy.

I see them relax.

Often new customers just stop by to say hi and get to know me, then we set an appointment.

TELLING A BOOK BY ITS COVER

The worst thing I ever saw in the hair care business was a prejudgment of a woman.

I was a consultant at a large salon, where I was to be their special stylist for a week.

The very first client which walked in was a lady with a big handbag which was old and beaten up, with socks rolled over her older farm shoes and her hair bunched up in a rubber band pony tail on top of her head.

The salon had advertised a special on a perm for $8.95, and the lady asked if someone could help her with a perm.

The manager looked at Jim, but Jim walked around the counter, not wanting the client.

I followed him, "I see you only have one customer scheduled today, why didn't you take the lady?"

"Ahhh, she's just here for the special."

"Let's see how this works out," I said.

Next the manager moved the woman to Sue.

"Hi, you are fortunate today because we have Mr. Guido here from Italy, and he can give you his opinion on your hair."

I spent time with her, and Sue did the work. I found her to be a wonderful lady.

She purchased the best perm we offered, and shampoos and con- ditioners to take home. Purchases totaled over $100 in 1966 dollars, which would be the equivalent of $300+ today.

And she looked great.

She insisted on giving me a $10 tip, and she paid from a large roll of mixed $50's and $20's.

A HAIRCUT FOR SAMMY
(As related by M.J. Parri)

Several years ago when our son Samuel Joseph Parri, Jr. (we call him Sammy) was about two years old, my husband Sam and I figured it was time for his first haircut. Our daughter Nina, who has beautiful hair, had no problem going to the salon to get pampered and have her hair trimmed, and we figured the same would hold true for Sammy.

Sammy however, turned what should be a simple task into the most torturing and painstaking experience ever. Getting his haircut was horrifying to him. His bone-chilling screams made it impossible for a set of shears to come next to his head. The ladies at the salon looked at me as if to say, "he's so cute with long hair – really- is it worth all the anguish your son is going through?" Even my salon stylist could not bring herself to attempt a hair cut on Sammy, since it was too upsetting for both of them.

Sam, my husband, suggested we take Sammy to a man's salon. However, Sammy remained consistent with his cries and screams of wanting to leave. After hearing suggestions from all of my friends and going to several places that used different tactics to entice a child to sit still, none had worked. Even, "...have your child sit on a wooden horse and watch a cartoon video," didn't do the trick.

Then, one day something made me open the yellow pages and look for a salon with a "catchy advertisement or a gimmick." Then I stumbled upon "Guido's." Forget the gimmick, I thought to myself– why didn't I think of this before? I need an Italian! Guido will know what to do. Even though I didn't know Guido, I had a good feeling about him.

I took Sammy to Guido's without prepping him that it was haircut time. I knew Sammy would get the picture as soon as he saw the dreadful scissors, and prepared myself for the usual screams. As soon as we met Guido, we felt we were "at home." You actually were in Guido's home, where his salon is located.

After letting Sammy explore the salon for a moment, while I gave Guido a little heads up regarding our prior experiences. Guido in his most calming and relaxing voice said, "No problem."

He patted the swivel chair and asked Sammy to climb up in the big mans seat...I can't even tell you what they talked about, but Guido had a conversation with Sammy the entire time. They were bonding. I did hear Guido tell Sammy, "You're a handsome boy, Sammy." I loved Guido immediately! And in the small world in which we live, my conversation with Guido that day proved that Sam and I already knew two of his brothers, Leo and Nick.

Sammy is now 14, and it has been many years since his first haircut with Guido.

Both he and Sam see Guido for a good cut and a great conversation on a regular basis. We have met all of Guido's family over the years, and have always been treated with love and affection— there is no other way with the Cornacchione's.

If it were not for Sammy's hair cutting thrills, we may have never met one of our dearest friends- Guido.

ZEBRA HAIR

A young woman came into the salon with her boyfriend, saying she wanted the ZEBRA LOOK.

This was in the 1970's, and the boyfriend wanted the hair bright orange, and she had dark hair, so when it grew out, it would look like an orange zebra.

He was here from the army, and planned to leave in a week to go back.

At first, I couldn't understand why they wanted such a weird look.

I tried talking them out of it, and explained what it would look like when it grew out.

Other customers who overheard were outraged, and didn't believe I'd do it.

I had to explain to the other customers that the couple was my client, and I had to give them the service they wanted.

When it was all done, I asked the two why they wanted to do it.

"When we go to Long Island, NY, to see her grandmother, man, she is going to s—t when she sees this."

RECIPES

BASIC TOMATO SAUCE

1/2 cup extra-virgin olive oil
2 cloves garlic, chopped
1 small onion, chopped
1 carrot, chopped
1 celery stalk, chopped
1/2 teaspoon salt
1/4 teaspoon ground black pepper
1 teaspoon dried basil
1 teaspoon dried parsley
2 dried bay leaves
2 (32-ounce) cans crushed tomatoes
1-4 tablespoons unsalted butter, if needed

Directions

In a large sauce pan, heat olive oil over medium high heat for about a minute. Add onion and garlic, saute until soft and translucent for approximately 5 minutes. Next add celery, carrots, salt and pepper. Saute until all the vegetables are soft, approximately 5 more minutes. Add crushed tomatoes, basil, parsley, and bay leaves and simmer uncovered on low heat for about 1-1 1/2 hours. Remove bay leaves.

**If sauce tastes acidic, add 1 tablespoon of unsalted butter at a time (up to about 3 tablespoons), tasting after each tablespoon until flavor is to your liking.

**If desire smoother sauce, blend sauce in food processor.

EGGPLANT PARMIGIANA

Vegetable oil for frying
1 medium eggplant
1/2 cup all purpose flour for dredging
About 1 ½ cups seasoned breadcrumbs
4 large eggs beaten
1 cup Parmesan cheese
Salt and pepper
6 cups tomato sauce
8 ounces of shredded mozzarella

Directions

Preheat oven to 350 degrees F and heat about 1/2 cup oil in a large pan.

Peel the eggplant and slice into ¼ inch-thick round slices.

Place the flour and breadcrumbs in a medium bowl. In another medium bowl, whisk the eggs and 1/3 cup Parmesan cheese . Dip an eggplant slice in the egg, and then dredge it in the breadcrumb mixture. Shake off any excess breading and place the eggplant in the hot oil and fry until golden brown on both sides, about 2-3 mins. Repeat with the remaining eggplant.

Once all of the eggplant has been fried, get a rectangular baking pan and start layering the eggplant. First, cover the bottom of the baking pan (about 15 x 10 x 2 inch) with 1/3 inch of sauce. Arrange half the eggplant over the sauce. Cover eggplant with another 1/3 of sauce. Sprinkle half of the Parmesan left, and half of the mozzarella over the sauced eggplant. Repeat with the remaining eggplant, sauce, parmesan, and mozzarella. Bake until hot and just beginning to brown, about 30 minutes. Serve immediately.

RACK OF LAMB WITH PESTO

3 racks of lamb (yields 6 servings), trimmed
1/3 cup extra-virgin olive oil, plus 2-3 tablespoons
1/2 tsp salt and ground black pepper, and extra for seasoning
2 gloves garlic
1 1/2 cup fresh mint leaves
1 cup fresh basil leaves
1/2 cup toasted walnuts
3 tablespoons grated Parmesan cheese
2 tablespoons fresh lemon juice or more to liking

Blend mint, basil, nuts, cheese, and lemon juice, garlic, salt & pepper in a food processor until mixed. With machine running, slowly add 1/3 cup olive oil until mixture is smooth and creamy.

Sprinkle racks of lamb with salt and pepper to liking. Heat 2 tablespoons of olive oil in a large heavy skillet over high heat. Place 1 rack in skillet at a time and sear until nice and brown about 3-5 minutes per side. Transfer lamb racks to a baking sheet when done searing each one and let cool down to room temp about 10- 15 minutes.

Slice the racks of lamb into lamb rib chops. Sprinkle individual lamb chops with a little olive oil and salt and pepper. Preheat grill to 400F. Arrange lamb chops in a single layer on grill. Grill lamb chops to desired doneness, about 3 minutes per each side for medium rare.

Serve 2-3 lamb chops with a spoon of pesto spread on top.

BOLOGNESE SAUCE

Ingredients

1/4 cup extra-virgin olive oil
Salt and freshly ground black pepper
1 medium onion, coarsely chopped
2 garlic cloves, peeled and coarsely chopped
1/4 cup flat-leaf Italian parsley, chopped
5-6 fresh basil leaves, chopped
1 celery stalk, coarsely chopped
1 carrot, coarsely chopped
1 pound ground chuck beef
1 (28-ounce) can crushed tomatoes

Directions

Heat the olive oil in a large skillet. Add the onion and garlic and saute over medium heat until the onions become soft and translucent about 7-8 minutes. Add the celery and carrot and saute for 5 minutes. Add the ground beef and brown over slightly higher heat. Cook until meat is no longer pink, about 9-10 minutes. Add the crushed tomatoes, parsley and basil and cook over medium low heat until the sauce thickens about 30 mins.. Season with salt and pepper to taste.

ZUPPA DI PISELLI CON POMODORO
(split pea soup with tomatoes)

2 cups green split pea lentils (picked over and rinsed)
2 medium fresh tomatoes chopped
1 celery stalk, coarsely chopped
2 carrots, coarsely chopped
2 cups frozen or fresh broccoli, coarsely chopped
2 chicken cubes
8 cups water
salt and pepper

Directions

Add all ingredients together in a large soup pan. Cook about one hour and 15 minutes over medium heat or until lentils and vegetables are tender.

Add water to dilute if too thick or strong at end. Season with salt and pepper to taste.

POLLO CON PASTA ALLA SICILIANA
(chicken strips with pasta, Sicilian style)

3 chicken breasts with bone
1/2 cup flour
3 tbsp olive oil
1 lb. spaghetti
8 cups water
1 tbsp salt
1 chicken bouillon crushed
1/2 cup Parmesan cheese

Directions

Debone the chicken and cut chicken breasts into 3/4 inch slices. Set aside.

Boil bones and skin of chicken in water and salt for about one hour. Strain broth and place back on stove to a simmer boil. Add crushed chicken bouillon.

Heat oil in fry pan. Sprinkle chicken slices with salt and pepper. Dredge chicken strips in flour and fry until golden brown about 3-4 mins. Place cooked chicken strips in chicken stock and repeat with rest of chicken strips. Allow broth with chicken strips to boil down for about 10 mins. until slightly thickened.

Prepare spaghetti noodles according to package directions al dente (slightly firm). Place a serving of spaghetti in a bowl with a scoop of broth and a few chicken strips. Top with Parmesan cheese to taste.

STEWED ZUCCHINI AND TOMATOES

2 small zucchinis, cut in half then sliced in half moons
1 medium size onion, cut in half then sliced thinly
2 medium tomatoes, chopped
2 tbsp olive oil
4 fresh basil leaves, chopped
salt and pepper

Directions:

In a large skillet, saute onions in olive oil until translucent about 8 mins. Then, add zucchini and tomatoes. Season with salt and pepper. Cook for another 15-20 mins. or until tender. Add fresh basil and cook another 1-2 mins. Serve hot as a side dish or over rice.

PASTA NCASCIATA
(Sicilian-style layered pasta)

6 cups Bolognese sauce
2 tbsps olive oil
1 cup breadcrumbs, seasoned
1 lb. penne pasta
green fennel stems from one bulb, chopped
1 cup mozzarella cheese, shredded
1 cup Parmesan or Romano grated cheese plus 2 tbsps.

Directions:

Preheat oven to 375 F.

Boil penne pasta according to package directions for half the time suggested (pasta will be very firm and cook rest of way in oven) and set aside in bowl.

Bring small pan of salted water to a boil. Add fennel stems and cook about 3-5 mins until slightly tender. Set aside.

Heat olive oil in pan over medium heat. Add breadcrumbs and stir until breadcrumbs lightly toasted about 2-3 mins. Set aside.

Cover the bottom of a rectangular pan (about 14" x 9"x 2") with 2 cups of sauce. Place 1/2 of pasta over sauce. Sprinkle half the breadcrumbs on top of pasta. Layer half the fennel on top of breadcrumbs. Sprinkle half of mozzarella cheese on top of fennel. Sprinkle half of the Parmesan cheese on top of fennel.

Cover with another 2 cups of sauce and form another layer with pasta, breadcrumbs, fennel, mozzarella cheese, and Parmesan cheese. Top with last 2 cups of sauce.

Sprinkle with last 2 tbsps. cheese. Bake in oven uncovered for about 20 mins. Serve hot.

FRITTATA WITH ZUCCHINI FLOWERS

6 large eggs
1/4 cup heavy cream
1/4 cup grated parmesan cheese
pinch of salt and fresh ground pepper
2 tablespoons chopped fresh basil
4 zucchini flowers roughly chopped
4 tablespoons olive oil

Directions:

Preheat oven to broil setting.

Beat eggs, cream, grated cheese, salt & pepper, and basil together in bowl.

Heat the oil in a heavy ovenproof 9-12 inch skillet pan. Sauté the zucchini flowers for 2-3 minutes.

Stir egg mixture into skillet and cook on medium-low heat until egg mixture is almost set (about 3-5 minutes). Then place skillet under the broiler and cook until golden brown about another 3 minutes.

Remove from pan. Cut into 6-8 pieces.

PIZZA DOUGH

2 1/4 teaspoons yeast
1/2 teaspoon brown sugar
1 1/2 cups warm water (110F)
1 teaspoon salt
2 tablespoons olive oil
3 1/3 cups bread flour
1 tablespoon cornmeal

Directions:

In large bowl dissolve yeast and brown sugar in water. Let sit for 10 minutes.

Stir in salt and oil to yeast solution.

Mix 2 1/2 cups of flour.

Turn dough onto well floured surface and knead in more flour until it is no longer sticky.

Let dough rise until double (about 1-2 hours).

Punch down dough and form into 2 tight balls.

Allow dough to relax about 5-10 minutes before rolling out.

Roll out, add sauce and toppings. Then bake on preheated pizza stone sprinkled with 1 tablespoon of cormeal at 500F for 10-12 minutes.

ORANGE-PISTACHIO BISCOTTI

1 3/4 cups all-purpose flour
1/2 teaspoon baking soda
1/2 teaspoon baking powder
1/2 cup unsalted butter at room temp
Grated zest from 1 orange
1 cup sugar
1 1/2 teaspoons vanilla extract
2 eggs
1 cup salted shelled pistachio nuts

Directions:

Sift together flour, baking soda, & baking powder into a bowl; set aside.

Beat butter, sugar, orange zest, & vanilla in a large bowl until light and fluffy. Slowly mix in eggs, beating well after adding each one. Stir in pistachios. Then add the flour mixture and mix just until incorporated. Cover with plastic wrap and refrigerate until chilled (about an hour or so).

Divide the dough in half. Roll each half into a log about 1 1/2 inches in diameter. Place on a greased and floured baking sheet side-by-side about 6 inches apart.

Bake at 350F until light brown or about 25 minutes. The logs will spread while baking. Remove baking sheet from oven and allow to cool slightly (about 10-15 minutes).

Using a knife, cut the logs into slices about 3/4 inch thick. Arrange the slices cut-side down on the baking sheet. Bake another 15 minutes or until golden brown. Transfer biscotti to wire racks to cool.

You can store these in freezer bags and place in freezer for months.

They also taste great dipped in melted semi-sweet chocolate for an elegant touch.

POACHED PEARS IN RED WINE WITH MASCARPONE FILLING

6 firm Bosc or Bartlett pears
1 bottle red wine
1/2 whole vanilla bean
2 cinnamon sticks
1 1/2 cup sugar
8 ounces mascarpone cheese softened
1/4 heavy cream
1/4 cup powdered sugar
2 tablespoons crushed toasted almonds (optional)

Directions:

Peel pears and leave stems intact. In a large saucepan, bring wine and an equal amount of cold water to simmer (empty wine from bottle in pan & then fill bottle with cold water and pour into pan). Split vanilla bean lengthwise and add to wine and water mixture.

Add cinnamon sticks and sugar to taste. Add pears to liquid and simmer over medium heat for about 45 minutes or until pears are tender. Cool pears in wine mixture to room temp. You can refrigerate them in wine mixture until you are ready to fill them. The longer they soak in mixture the deeper red color the pears become.

Slice small stem portion from pears and set stems aside. Core pears with an apple corer, leaving pear whole.

Whisk together mascarpone cheese, heavy cream, pinch of cinnamon and powdered sugar until smooth. Add almonds if desired. Transfer to a pastry bag (or ziploc bag & then cut small piece from corner of bag). Pipe filling into pears and finish by putting stems gently on top of mascarpone filling on top of pear.

Bring 2 cups of remaining wine liquid to a simmer and reduce by half. Cool to room temp. Spoon generously over pears.

ITALIAN WEDDING SOUP

For Broth:

1 small whole chicken (gizzards removed) or half chicken with bone in
1 medium onion
1 whole carrots
2 bay leaves
1 stalk of celery
10 cups water
2 chicken bouillons

Directions:

Bring to a boil over medium-high heat, skimming foam off of the top as it forms.

When the water comes to a boil, adjust the heat so the broth cooks at a steady gentle boil. Cook for 1 1/2 hours.

Check to make sure chicken is cooked through. Strain broth through fine colander or cheesecloth. Set the chicken aside to cool down to room temp. Add salt or chicken bouillons to broth to taste.

Shred cooled chicken into pieces and place in bowl. Cover so chicken won't dry out. Discard skin and bones.

(See following page for meatballs, and rest of recipe)

ITALIAN WEDDING SOUP-CONTINUED

For meatballs:

1 lb. ground meat
2/3 cup ground seasoned breadcrumbs
1 egg
1/4 cup Parmesan cheese
Salt and ground pepper

Directions:

For the meatballs, place the meat, bread crumbs, parsley, Parmesan cheese, egg, 1 teaspoon salt, and 1/2 teaspoon pepper in a bowl and combine gently with a fork. With a teaspoon, form 1-inch diameter meatballs and drop into pan of broth while gently boiling.

For rest of soup:

1 head of escarole cleaned and roughly chopped
2 carrots chopped
2 celery stalks chopped
1 pound of pastina (like acini di pepe)

Directions:

Once meatballs have been placed in broth, add escarole, carrots, and celery. Cook for another 30 mins. or until vegetables are soft. Once vegetables and meatballs are cooked through, add pastini and shredded chicken. Cook until pastina is al dente (or slightly firm), about 5-7 mins.

MAGIC CHEESE
(homemade cheese)

Ingredients:

3 tbsp. vegetable oil

2-3 tbsp. salt

1 gallon of milk (yields 2 baskets of cheese)

4-6 ounces of white vinegar

2 miniature cheese baskets or colanders (2 cheese baskets the size of a cereal bowl)

TIPS TO PREVENT MILK FROM STICKING BEFORE STARTING:

1. Add water to the pot and swirl the water around to cover all sides. Then dump the water out.

2. Add vegetable oil to the rim of the pot. (This prevents milk from boiling over).

Directions:

Add 3 tbsp. vegetable oil to a stainless steel pot, after rinsing and drying the pot.

Coat inside rim with oil as in "Tips" above. Turn stove on to med-high temp.

Add 1 gallon of milk to pan (whole milk will produce more, but any type will do). Add 2–3 tablespoons of salt to pan. Bring milk to a full boil (usually 13 minutes).

Once the milk is boiling, reduce heat to low. Add 4-6 ounces of white vinegar, and turn the heat OFF. Milk will begin to curdle and is now forming "the cheese" at the top surface. Using a large slotted spoon, skim the cheese from the top surface.

Fill your 2 baskets with the curdles, pressing down firmly to pack the cheese and squeeze out excess liquids. Allow the molds to set for approximately 2–3 minutes. Turn upside down on a decorative plate and tap the basket to release the cheese.

Serve with your favorite crackers, sliced tomatoes, or fruit and don't forget the wine!

Variations: add bits of chives, pieces of sundried tomatoes, chopped jalapeño pepper, or seasonings as you are filling your baskets in between each spoonful.

THE FOUNTAIN/
LA FONTANA

THE FOUNTAIN/ LA FONTANA

Little Vincenza had adored fountains from the time she was a little girl.

When walking in the town of Bronte Provincia Catania in Sicily with her father, she would marvel at the three-tiered fountain at the center of town with the water gracefully draping from the sides, and splashing into a pool in which she would let her fingers play.

When older and married to Guido, her dream of the fountain returned. "Guido, I would like a fountain," she said soon after they had moved into their home by the lake.

Every year, she would suggest that she desired a fountain, and Guido always replied that they would certainly have one.

Guido's plan was hidden to all.

He poured the cement base when Vincenza was at work, and covered all the fountain's pieces under tarps. The assembly of the fountain was done with Vincenza in the house, under the ruse they were waiting to leave for a party.

He came to her with a blindfold.

"Put this on," he said.

"I can't see with the blindfold on!," she replied.

He carefully guided her steps and took her to the raised platform surrounded by plantings, placed in front of the home so all could see.

Vincenza opened her eyes to find a gigantic three-tiered fountain, water flowing from all sides into a generous base.

"Ooooh, Guido, this is nice. How did you do it so I didn't see?"

He explained all the steps he'd taken to hide the project's progress as it came from an idea in his mind- based on her hopes and dreams, to the working fountain.

Perhaps it is worth remembering that for each of us, our dreams seem to lay unfulfilled...yet who knows what powers are at work to bring these, our dreams, to fruition on a day which will come as a complete surprise.

The Fountain/ La Fontana